AUSTRALIAN HOMESCHOOLING SERIES

Successful Spelling 8

9TH IN A SERIES

Years 8 – 10

CORONEOS PUBLICATIONS

Item No 569

This book is available from recognised booksellers or contact:

Coroneos Publications

Telephone: (02) 9838 9265   **Facsimile:** (02) 9838 8982
Business Address: 2/195 Prospect Highway Seven Hills 2147
Website: www.coroneos.com.au
E-mail: info@fivesenseseducation.com.au

Item # 569
Successful Spelling 8
by Valerie Marett
First published 2019

ISBN: 978-1-922034-78-6
© Valerie Marett

Contents

Australian Homeschooling #569
Successful Spelling 8

Notes to Parents

This is the 9th in a series of spelling books designed to improve both the students' spelling and vocabulary. Do not attempt this book before completing *Successful Spelling 7.*

A student should leave school with at least a 4,000 word vocabulary. This series will help ensure this. *Test Your Spelling 5 & 6 or Test Your Spelling 7 & 8* will ensure correct placement in this series.

It is essential to learn to spell well. To spell well it is important to have mastered the phonetical sounds and have a logical spelling programme that reinforces the sounds that have been learnt. If a phonics programme has not been used, ensure your child works through *Phonics Revision Workbooks 1-4* and *Successful Spelling 7* first.

Most spelling units have been grouped into common sounds, prefixes or suffixes to make learning the words easier. **Each unit is for one week.**

To get the best from this book:
- have your child read aloud the spelling words for the week.
- each week the child should look up the definition of each word.
- over the period of a week the child should write a sentence using each word.
- The child should memorise the words. The best way to do this is to write them out at least once a day, saying the word and sounding it as they are being written. (Dividing the word into syllables will help spell and pronounce the words correctly.)
- the child should complete all exercises.
- the child should learn the meaning of any prefixes or suffixes given in the exercises.
- the child should learn any spelling rules.
- at the end of the week an adult should test the child's spelling words. All words incorrectly spelt should be rewritten correctly three times and added to the following week's list.
- If more than five words in any week are spelt wrong it is suggested the unit be repeated.
- When the book is completed a parent should give the final spelling test.

Unit 1: -ity

Look up the meaning and then learn these words.

affinity	alacrity	austerity
authenticity	congruity	disparity
duplicity	equanimity	gullibility
illogicality	longevity	perversity
probity	proclivity	solemnity

Etymology or Word Origin—equanimity

The word comes from the Latin *aequanimitatem* "evenness of mind, calmness;" and from *aequanimis* "mild, kind," also from *aequus* "even, level. " It was used in the English language from 1610s.

The suffix -ity makes an abstract noun from an adjective and means "condition or quality of being what the adjective describes." Equanimity means being equal.

A. Look carefully at each word below. Write the adjectival form of the word. The first one is completed for you. Use a dictionary if you need to.

1. authenticity	authentic		2. illogicality	_____
3. austerity	_____		4. longevity	_____
5. solemnity	_____		6. disparity	_____
7. gullibility	_____		8. congruity	_____
9. perversity	_____		10. equanimity	_____

B. Write the definition of the following words.

1.   affinity: _____

    _____

2.   proclivity: _____

    _____

3.   probity: _____

    _____

4.   congruity: _____

    _____

A. Write a synonym and an antonym in the column provided. Do not just choose the simplest words you can find.

	Synonym	Antonym
1. duplicity	_____	_____
2. perversity	_____	_____
3. congruity	_____	_____
4. probity	_____	_____
5. alacrity	_____	_____

B. Choose a word from your spelling list to match the definition.

1. long life; long service _____

2. easily tricked or manipulated into a situation _____

3. sternness or severity of manner or attitude _____

4. a deliberate desire to behave in an unreasonable or unacceptable way _____

5. a great difference, inconsistency _____

6. deceitfulness, dishonesty, deception _____

7. genuine, real _____

8. brisk and cheerful readiness _____

C. Divide the following words into syllables. Remember, <u>every syllable must contain a vowel.</u> Dividing words into syllables helps with spelling a word.

1. authenticity _____   2. disparity _____

3. equanimity _____   4. gullibility _____

D. Prefixes can provide a clue to the meaning of a word. Use your dictionary to find the meaning of the following prefixes that can be found in your spelling list.

1. pro:_____

2. dis: _____

3. per: _____

© Valerie Marett
Coroneos Publications

Australian Homeschooling #569
Successful Spelling 8

Unit 2: -ory, -ogy, -ary

Look up the meaning and then learn these words.

conciliatory	cursory	derogatory
desultory	expository	illusory
peremptory	histology	ideology
morphology	ophthalmology	pathology
tautology	complementary	complimentary
corollary	quandary	rudimentary

Etymology or Word Origin—peremptory

The word comes from the Latin *peremptorius* "destructive, decisive, final," from *peremptor* "destroyer," from *perimpere* "destroy, cut off." When referring to a person or their words it means "certain, assured, brooking no debate."

A. When you see words ending in "–ology" it usually but not always means "the study of" a subject. Look at each word below. Write what it is the study of.

1. ophthalmology: _____

2. histology: _____

3. morphology: _____

4. pathology: _____

   _____

B. <u>**Words ending in -*ory* can be nouns (e.g., *category,*) or adjectives (e.g., *derogatory*.)**</u> **Say whether each word below is a noun or an adjective.**

1. expository _____   2. conciliatory _____

3. desultory _____   4. tautology _____

5. illusory _____   6. history _____

C. Write the definition of each of the words below. Write a sentence showing you understand how to use the word.

1. complementary: _____

   _____

2. complimentary: _____

   _____

A. Choose a word from your list to fit each definition below.

1. hasty; not thorough or detailed   _____

2. relating to an immature, undeveloped or basic form   _____

3. a phrase or expression in which the same thing is said twice in different words   _____

4. a statement that follows with little or no proof required from an already proven statement   _____

5. occurring randomly or occasionally; lacking a plan, purpose or enthusiasm   _____

6. a state of perplexity or uncertainty over what to do in a difficult situation   _____

B. Words ending in -ary can be nouns (e.g., *boundary*,) adjectives (e.g., *ordinary*,) or both (e.g., *contemporary*.)

Beside each word below write whether the word is a noun, or an adjective. Use a dictionary to help you.

1. complimentary   _____   2. quandary   _____

3. corollary   _____   4. rudimentary _____

5. complementary   _____   6. ideology   _____

C. The words below are missing their endings. Add -ary, -ory, -ogy or -ity to complete the words.

1. liter _____   2. laborat_____   3. necess_____

4. anthropol_____   5. dormit_____   6. abnormal_____

7. milit_____   8. archaeol_____   9. civil_____

D. A synonym of one of your list words is written below. Write the list word.

1. rapid   _____   2. uncompromising _____

3. disparaging_____   4. basic   _____

5. haphazard _____   6. placating   _____

Unit 3: y says ee

Look up the meaning and then learn these words.

calumny	clemency	consistency
controversy	delinquency	dichotomy
discrepancy	elegy	entreaty
hegemony	hierarchy	ignominy
oxymoron	pithy	soliloquy trichotomy

Remember: <u>when y is the only vowel at the end of a word of more than one syllable it has a long e sound.</u>

Etymology or Word Origin—calumny
Calumny comes from the Latin *calumnia* "trickery, subterfuge, misrepresentation, malicious charge," and from *calvi* "to trick, deceive." Calumny means false & malicious misrepresentation of the words or actions of others, calculated to injure their reputation.

A. Divide each word below into syllables.

1. elegy _____

2. pithy _____

3. trichotomy _____

4. delinquency _____

5. discrepancy _____

6. ignominy _____

B. Write the adjectival form of each word below.

1. hierarchy _____

2. clemency _____

3. discrepancy _____

4. hegemony _____

5. ignominy _____

6. discrepancy _____

C. Change the following nouns to verbs.

1. calumny _____

2. entreaty _____

3. consistency _____

D. Find the meaning of the following prefixes.

1. con: _____

2. tri: _____

3. en—: _____

N.B. Con- comes before c, d, f, g, j, n, q, s, t, v and sometimes before vowels.

A. Choose a word from your list to fit each definition below.

1. leadership or dominance, especially by one state over another _____

2. a figure of speech in which apparently contradictory terms appear in conjunction _____

3. public shame or disgrace _____

4. minor crime, especially that committed by young people, neglect of one's duty _____

5. repeated branching into two equal parts _____

6. an act of speaking one's thoughts aloud when by oneself or regardless of any hearers, especially by a character in a play. _____

7. a poem of serious reflection, typically a lament for the dead _____

8. the system in which members of an organization or society are ranked according to status or authority _____

9. a division into three categories _____

B. Provide an antonym for each word below.

1. clemency _____   2. discrepancy _____

3. controversy _____   4. consistency _____

5. entreaty _____

C. Find a synonym from your spelling list for the following words.

1. infamy, obloquy _____

2. difference, disparity, variance _____

3. slander, slur, aspersion _____

4. aside, say to oneself _____

5. meaningful, substantial _____

© Valerie Marett
Coroneos Publications

Australian Homeschooling #569
Successful Spelling 8

Unit 4: y says short i; y says long i

Look up the meaning and then learn these words.

acronym	androgynous	aneurysm	cataclysm
cryptic	cynicism	dysfunctional	eponym
idiosyncratic	idyllic	mythology	pseudonym
synecdoche	synecology		
cyclical	dynamic	paroxysm	stereotype
vilify			

Etymology or Word Origin—cataclysm

Cataclysm comes from the Greek *kataklysmos* "deluge, flood, inundation;" from *kataklyzein* "to deluge," and from *kata* "down" + *klyzein* "to wash."

A. Choose a word from the spelling list to fit each definition below.

1. a figure of speech in which a part is made to represent the whole   _____

2. a person after whom a discovery, place, invention etc. is named   _____

3. sudden attack or outburst of rage or laughter   _____

4. excessive localized enlargement of an artery   _____

5. an inclination to believe people are motivated by self-interest, skepticism   _____

6. ecological study of plant or animal communities   _____

7. neither distinctly male or distinctly female, with stamen and pistils in the same flower   _____

8. anything highly individualized or eccentric   _____

9. a fictitious name, especially one assumed by an author   _____

10. violent upheaval, especially social or political   _____

B. Fill in each blank below with the form of the word requested.

1. vilify   _____(n)   2. idyllic (n)   _____

3. cryptic _____ (adv)   4. mythology (adj) _____

A. Write the adjectival form of the following words.

1. stereotype _____
2. aneurysm _____
3. mythology _____
4. cataclysm _____
5. eponym _____
6. cynicism _____

B. Write the noun form of these words.

1. cyclical _____
2. vilify _____
3. idyllic _____
4. dynamic _____

C. Find and write the meaning of these prefixes. Prefixes help us understand the meaning of the word.

1. an- _____

2. crypto- _____

3. pseudo- _____

4. dys- _____

5. cata- _____

6. ac- _____

7. syn- _____

8. dynam- _____

D. Find and write the meaning of these suffixes. Suffixes help us understand the meaning of the word.

1. -ism _____

2. -ic _____

3. -ology _____

4. -onym _____

E. Divide these words into syllables.

1. dysfunctional _____
2. idiosyncratic _____
3. androgynous _____
4. synecology _____

Unit 5: Revision

Revise these words.

aneurysm	authenticity	cataclysm	complementary
controversy	corollary	derogatory	desultory
duplicity	gullibility	ignominy	oxymoron
paroxysm	peremptory	perversity	proclivity
pseudonym	rudimentary	soliloquy	stereotype

A. Complete the rules below.

1. The suffix –ity makes an _____ from an _____.

2. Every syllable must _____.

3. When y is the _____ vowel at the end of a word of more than _____ syllable it has a _____.

4. Words ending in -ology usually mean _____.

B. Look at the words below. Each is a synonym of one of your spelling words, not always the most common. Write the matching spelling word in the space.

1. classify _____   2. non de plume _____

3. credibility _____   4. purposeless _____

5. vestigial _____   6. naiveness _____

7. catastrophe _____   8. decisive _____

9. contention _____   10. deceit _____

C. Look at the words below. Each is a antonym of one of your spelling words, not always the most common. Write the matching spelling word in the space.

1. accord _____   2. geniality _____

3. incompatible _____   4. complimentary _____

5. honour _____   6. detestation _____

D. On a separate sheet of paper make at least 60 smaller words from the word "complementary," e.g., come, late. **See if you can find more words than I found.**

A. Complete the crossword using the clues below. You will find all the words required in your spelling list.

Across

2. insult, involving disagreement or discredit
5. disconnected, going from one subject to another
6. one of two things that go together
7. credulous, easily persuaded
8. tendency or inclination
9. violent upheaval, especially social or political

Down

1. a prolonged argument or dispute, especially when conducted in public
3. genuine, of undisputed origin
4. an image of a particular person or thing that has become fixed through being widely held

B. Rewrite the following words as plurals.

1. proclivity _____   2. oxymoron _____

C. Revise the rules for changing nouns ending in "y" to plural by filling in the blanks below with the correct words.

When nouns end in y and are proceeded by a vowel, to form a plural _____

_____. When nouns end in y and are proceeded by a consonant _____

_____. When proper nouns end in "y" the plural is formed

by adding _____.

Unit 6: -tion

Look up the meaning and then learn these words.

aberration	abrogation	adjuration	adulation
approbation	asphyxiation	attrition	circumlocution
compunction	conflagration	contradiction	depreciation
depredation	derogation	diminution	equivocation
exemplification	gesticulation	homogenisation	improvisation

The suffix –tion is more commonly used than -sion. It indicates an act or process, a state or condition. If the base word ends with "t" or "te" then –tion will be used.

Etymology or Word Origin—circumlocution
Circumlocution comes from Latin *circumlocutionem* meaning "a speaking around" (the topic), from *circum-* meaning" around" + *locutionem meaning* "speaking."

A. The prefix ab– means "away from" or "off." Write the words from your spelling list that contain this prefix.

1. _____   2. _____

B. Find the meaning of the following prefixes and learn them. (Dictionaries often show the meaning of prefixes and suffixes.)

1. ad-, ap-: _____

2. com-, con-: _____

3. de-: _____

4. equi-: _____

5. gest-: _____

6. homo-: _____

7. in-, im-: _____

C. Write the base word for the following spelling words.

1. depreciation _____   2. improvisation _____

3. abrogation _____   4. homogenization _____

A. The first column contains the definition. The second column contains a spelling word that has been scrambled. Write the correct speling in the third column.

1. a solemn oath   tionjuraad   _____

2. a gesture instead of speaking   cugestitional   _____

3. an act of attacking or plundering   predtionade   _____

4. reducing someone's effectiveness
   through sustained attack   tionattri   _____

5. a lack of oxygen in the body leading
   to unconsciousness   phyxiationas   _____

6. prevarication, vagueness   caetionoquiv   _____

7. an extensive fire that destroys a
   great deal of land or property   racontionflag   _____

8. the repeal or abolition of a law
   right or agreement   tionroabga   _____

9. a feeling of guilt that follows doing
   something bad   punccomtion   _____

10. an exemption from or relaxation
    of a rule or law   adetionrog   _____

11. approval or praise   baprotionap   _____

12. a combination of ideas that are   dictiontracon   _____
    opposed to each other

13. something that is done
    spontaneously, especially in music   saprotionviim   _____

14. a reduction in size or importance   tiondiimun   _____

15. excessive admiration or praise   tionulaad   _____

B. Change the following words to a verb.

1. homogenisation   _____   2. exemplification   _____

3. improvisation   _____   4. gesticulation   _____

5. asphyxiation   _____   6. adjuration   _____

Unit 7: More -tion

Look up the meaning and then learn these words.

inauguration	injunction	inundation	invalidation
marginalisation	maturation	obfuscation	ossification
ostentation	personification	predilection	proliferation
requisition	sequestration	stagnation	summarisation
superannuation	trepidation	vituperation	volition

Etymology or Word Origin—proliferation
Proliferation comes from the Latin *proles* "offspring" + *ferre* "to bear, carry." Meaning "enlargement, extension, increase." From 1920 it was used especially of nuclear weapons.

A. Divide each word into syllables.

1. personification _____   2. superannuation _____

3. summarisation _____   4. predilection _____

5. sequestration _____   6. inauguration _____

B. Change the following spelling words to verbs.

1. marginalisation _____   2. inundation _____

3. ossification _____   4. stagnation _____

5. obfuscation _____   6. maturation _____

7. proliferation _____   8. invalidation _____

C. Change the following spelling words to adjectives.

1. ostentation _____   2. proliferation _____

3. inauguration _____   4. injunction _____

5. vituperation _____   6. invalidation_____

D. Unscramble the words below. They are taken from your spelling list.

1. quitionsire _____   2. tiontrepaid _____

3. iitonvol _____   4. valationidin _____

A. Choose a spelling word that is a synonym of the following words.

1. concise, succinct _____

2. voluntarily, freely _____

3. grandiose, pretentious _____

4. prohibition, ban, embargo _____

5. invective, disapprobation _____

6. request, appropriation _____

7. discredit, nullify _____

B. Write a spelling word that fits each description below.

1. an overwhelming abundance of people or things _____

2. making unclear or unintelligible _____

3. separating or taking legal possession of assets _____

4. a preference or special liking for something _____

5. the beginning or introduction of a policy or period _____

6. a feeling of fear or anxiety about something that might happen _____

7. hardening of tissue into a bony substance _____

8. rapid increase in the number or amount of something _____

9. regular payment into a fund towards a future pension _____

10. a figure intended to represent an abstract quality _____

11. the act of becoming fully developed _____

12. a prolonged period of little or no growth _____

13. the pretentious or showy display of wealth _____

14. bitter and abusive language _____

15. the faculty and power of using one's will _____

Unit 8: -city, -ly, -ally, -y says short i

Look up the meaning and then learn these words.

capacity	domesticity	eccentricity	egocentricity
ethnicity	felicity	ferocity	incapacity
paucity	perspicacity	specificity	tenacity
veracity		expeditiously	extensively
inquisitively	unashamedly	vehemently	vicariously
chronologically	sympathetically	labyrinth	misogynist

Etymology or Word Origin—veracity

Veracity comes from Medieval Latin *veracitatem* meaning "truthfulness," from Latin *verax* meaning "truthful," and from *verus* meaning "true."

A. Use your dictionary to help you fill in each blank below.

	Noun	Adjective	Adverb
1.	specificity	_____	_____
2.	egocentricity	_____	_____
3.	felicity	_____	_____
4.	veracity	_____	_____
5.	ethnicity	_____	_____
6.	perspicacity	_____	_____
7.	tenacity	_____	_____

B. Each word shown is an adverb. Complete the adjectival and noun form of each word.

		Adjective	Noun
1.	chronologically	_____	_____
2.	inquisitively	_____	_____
3.	vicariously	_____	_____
4.	expeditiously	_____	_____
5.	vehemently	_____	_____
6.	sympathetically	_____	_____

A. Choose a word from your spelling list that fits each definition below. Find the word in the wordsearch and highlight it.

C	A	P	A	C	I	T	Y	T	I	C	I	L	E	F
P	H	T	N	I	R	Y	B	A	L	S	S	M	P	Q
F	E	R	O	C	I	T	Y	T	I	C	A	R	E	V
M	I	S	O	G	Y	N	I	S	T	E	U	K	D	G
E	C	C	E	N	T	R	I	C	I	T	Y	T	G	A
X	Y	L	S	U	O	I	T	I	D	E	P	X	E	N
T	V	J	D	U	P	L	I	C	I	T	Y	X	J	E
E	E	U	Y	L	S	U	O	I	R	A	C	I	V	U
N	U	K	E	V	N	Y	N	G	G	B	T	Z	Q	R
S	Y	M	P	A	T	H	E	T	I	C	A	L	L	Y
I	Y	T	I	C	I	R	T	N	E	C	O	G	E	S
V	S	B	Y	L	D	E	M	A	H	S	A	N	U	M
E	I	N	Q	U	I	S	I	T	I	V	E	L	Y	N
L	G	Q	A	N	V	E	H	E	M	E	N	T	L	Y
Y	T	I	C	A	N	E	T	H	N	I	C	I	T	Y

1. conformity to facts; accuracy _____
2. a person who dislikes or is strongly prejudiced against women _____
3. the maximum amount something can contain _____
4. arranged in order of time _____
5. to do something forcefully and with emotion _____
6. the quality of being determined or persistent _____
7. having or regarding yourself as the centre of all things _____
8. being odd or capricious in behaviour or appearance _____
9. having a wide scope; far reaching _____
10. experiencing something through another person _____
11. intense happiness _____
12. a complicated network of passages or paths difficult to get out _____
13. belonging to a group with a common national tradition _____
14. a fierce or violent capacity _____

You will also find the words: expeditiously, inquisitively, unashamedly, sympathetically.

Unit 9: ph says the f sound

Look up the meaning and then learn these words.

apocryphal	atrophy	cacophonous	choreography
demographic	diaphanous	diphthong	emphatic
ephemeral	euphemism	euphonious	euphoria
neophyte	paraphernalia	periphery	phalanx
phenomena	phlegmatic	philanthropic	sophisticated
sycophant			

Etymology or Word Origin— cacophonous
This word came into use about 1650. Cacophonous comes from the Greek
kakophonos "harsh sounding," from *kakos* "bad, evil" + *phone* "voice, sound."

A. Write a spelling word that matches each definition.

1. charitable, seeking to promote the welfare of others _____

2. a mild or indirect word or expression substituted for
   one that is considered to be too harsh _____

3. a person who is new to a subject or activity _____

4. a bone of the finger or toe, a body of troops
   standing or moving in close formation _____

5. having an unemotional and stolidly calm disposition _____

6. the sequence of steps and movements in dance or
   figure skating, especially in a ballet or a staged dance _____

7. a person who acts obsequiously towards someone
   important in order to gain advantage _____

8. the outer limits or edge of an object _____

9. light, delicate and translucent _____

10. waste away, especially as a degeneration of the cells _____

11. pleasing to the ear _____

12. of doubtful authenticity although circulated as being
    true _____

A. <u>The prefix eu– comes from the Greek and means good, well, luckily, happily.</u> Write the 3 spelling words that contain the prefix eu–. Make sure you understand the meaning of the words.

1. _____   2. _____   3. _____

B. <u>The prefix dem– or demo– means people, populace, population.</u> Write a spelling word that contain the prefix dem–. Write 2 more words that contain the same prefix.

1. _____   2. _____   3. _____

C. <u>The suffixes -ous, -eous, -ose and -ious show the word is an adjective meaning having the quality of, relating to,</u>e.g.,adventurous. Write the 3 spelling words that contain this suffix.

1. _____   2. _____   3. _____

D. Divide the following words into syllables.

1. ephemeral _____   2. philanthropic _____

3. neophyte _____   3. paraphernalia _____

5. cacophonous_____   6. emphatic _____

7. apocryphal _____   8. periphery _____

E. Write the noun form of each adjective below.

1. cacophonous _____   2. philanthropic _____

3. apocryphal _____   4. demographic _____

5. phlegmatic _____   6. sophisticated _____

F. Write sentences using the word shown.

1. phlegmatic: _____

_____

2. euphemism: _____

_____

3. choreography: _____

_____

Unit 10: Revision

Revise these words.

aberration	abrogation	cacophonous	depreciation
diminution	duplicity	emphatic	expeditiously
ferocity	gesticulation	obfuscation	ostentation
periphery	phenomena	philanthropic	proliferation
sequestration	trepidation	vehemently	veracity

A. Complete the following.

1. The suffix –tion is more commonly used than _____. If the base word ends with _____ or _____ use -tion.

2. The prefix eu- comes from the Greek and means _____

    _____

3. The suffixes -ous, -eous, -ose and -ious show the word is an _____ meaning _____.

4. The prefix ab- means _____

5. The prefix dem- or demo- means _____

B. Many of our words come from Greek or Latin. Learn these common endings of plurals. Write the plural of each word. Sometimes "s" may also be used. Do not use this form here.

	Singular ending	Plural ending	Singular Form	Plural Form
1.	-a	-ae	alga	_____
2.	-on	-ona	phenomenon	_____
3.	-is	-es	parenthesis	_____
4.	-ex	-ices	index	_____
5.	-um	-a	medium	_____
6.	-us	-i	nucleus	_____

B. Divide the following words into syllables.

1. sequestration _____		2. phenomena _____
3. obfuscation _____		4. gesticulation _____

A. Use the clues to solve the crossword puzzle. It contains words from your spelling list.

Across

1. feeling of fear or alarm
3. rapid increase in the number or amount of something
5. savagery, brutality
6. the repeal or abolition of a law or agreement
7. an observable fact or occurrence
8. deceitfulness, perfidy

Down

2. benevolent, loving one's fellow humans
4. a departure from what is normal

B. Find three synonyms for each word below.

1. obfuscate _____

2. expeditiously _____

3. gesticulation _____

4. ostentation _____

Unit 11: -ial, -tial

Look up the meaning and then learn these words.

actuarial	adversarial	colloquial
congenial	conspiratorial	controversial
deferential	inconsequential	insubstantial
potential	precedential	preferential
proprietorial	quintessential	tangential
torrential		

Etymology or Word Origin: congenial
This word comes from the Latin *con-* "together" and *genialis* "of birth," and thus first meant "kindred." The sense of "agreeable" is first recorded 1711.

The prefix con– or com- can mean fully, e.g., conscious. **Con-, com- col- or coll-can also mean with or together,** e.g., converge, compact, collaborate.

A. In the space below write the spelling words that contain the prefixes con- or col-.

1. _____   2. _____   3. _____

4. _____

B. Write the meaning of each word in exercise A.

1. _____

2. _____

3. _____

4. _____

The prefix pre- means before, e.g., precede **and the prefix pro- means before or forward,** e.g., propel

C. In the space below write the spelling words that contain the prefix pre- or pro-.

1. _____   2. _____   3. _____

D. Homonyms are two or more words having the same spelling or pronunciation but having different meanings, e.g., bare, bear. One of the words in your spelling list is part of a homonym. Write it and the other homonym below.

1. _____   2. _____

A. Write a spelling word that would complete each sentence below.

1. The youngest son of the king received _____ treatment wherever he went.

2. While waiting for the bus they talked about _____ things.

3. The _____ ingredient in the pudding was the teaspoon of nutmeg.

4. The _____ of the energy source was unlimited.

5. Your essays should not contain any _____ expressions.

6. The topic of euthanasia is very _____.

7. The material contained is _____ and should not be photocopied or distributed.

8. The law system used in our courts is _____.

The prefixes im– or in– mean into, on, near, or towards, e.g., instead, import. **They can also mean not**, e.g., inviolate. impregnable.

B. In the space below write the spelling words that contain the prefix in–.

1. _____   2. _____

C. Choose a word from your spelling list to fit each definition below.

1. relating to the profession dealing with the assessment and management of risks of financial investments and insurance policies   _____

2. respectful, attentive, obsequious   _____

3. pleasing or liked on account of having qualities similar to one's own   _____

4. diverting from a previous course or line   _____

5. having or showing the capacity to develop into something in the future   _____

D Change each word to an adverb.

1. insubstantial _____   2. torrential _____

3. conspiratorial _____   4. colloquial _____

Unit 12: -ate

Look up the meaning and then learn these words.

acculturate	actuate	attenuate	baccalaureate
collaborate	commemorate	commensurate	conglomerate
contraindicate	corroborate	debilitate	decimate
defibrillate	delineate	denigrate	disparate
disseminate	dissipate	emulate	enervate
enumerate	exacerbate	expiate	expostulate

Etymology or Word Origin— conglomerate

This word comes from the Latin *conglomeratus*, "to roll together," from *com-* "together," from *glomerare* "to gather into a ball," and from *glomus* "a ball."

The prefixes dis- and dif- mean not, opposite of, reverse, separate, deprive of, away, e.g., disallow, differ.

A. In the space below write the spelling words that contain the prefix dis-.

1. _____ 2._____ 3. _____

B. Match a word from question A to each of the definitions below.

1. spread widely   _____

2. to cause something to spread out and disappear   _____

3. essentially different in kind; not easily compared _____

The prefix ex– means out of, away from, lacking or former, e.g., exit, exclusive.

C. Write each word starting with the prefix ex– from your spelling list. Write the definition of the word next to it.

1. _____

2. _____

3. _____

D. Divide each of the following words into syllables.

1. acculturate _____   2. corroborate _____

3. commensurate _____   4. emulate _____

A. Use your dictionary to complete the following chart.

	Noun	Adjective	Verb	Adverb
1.	_____	_____	collaborate	_____
2.	_____	_____	debilitate	
3.	_____		delineate	
4.	_____	_____	enumerate	
5.	_____	_____	attenuate	

B. Find a word from your spelling list that fits the following definition.

1. criticise, disparage unfairly _____

2. an examination intended to qualify students for higher education _____

3. make someone weak and infirm _____

4. assimilate to a different culture _____

5. match or surpass, typically by imitation _____

6. make someone act in a particular way; motivate _____

7. express strong disapproval or disagreement _____

8. describe or portray precisely _____

9. make feel drained of energy _____

10. suggest something shouldn't be used (usually medicine) _____

11. kill, destroy or lose a large proportion of _____

12. corresponding in size or degree; in proportion _____

C. Write the definition of the following spelling words:

1. attenuate: _____

2. exacerbate: _____

3. collaborate: _____

Unit 13: more -ate

Look up the meaning and then learn these words.

exonerate	expurgate	extricate	inchoate
indeterminate	indiscriminate	importunate	instigate
inveterate	obdurate	obviate	palliate
perpetuate	placate	prevaricate	promulgate
propitiate	relegate	satiate	scintillate
somnambulate	subjugate	substantiate	vacillate

Etymology or Word Origin— relegate

This word comes from the Latin *relegatus* "remove, dismiss, banish, send away, schedule, put aside," from *re-* "back" + *legare* "send with a commission." Meaning "place in a position of inferiority" is recorded from 1790.

The prefixes in-, im-, il- or ir– mean not, into, near or towards, e.g., instead, illegible, irresolute, import.

A. In the space below write the spelling words that contain the prefix in- or im-.

1. _____   2._____   3._____

4. _____   5._____   6._____

B. Write sentences using 3 of the spelling words from question A.

1. _____

2. _____

3. _____

C. Complete the chart by filling in the gaps with the appropriate word.

	Noun	Adjective	Verb	Adverb
1.	_____	_____	subjugate	
2.		_____	scintillate	_____
3.	_____	_____	expurgate	
4.	_____	_____	relegate	
5.	_____	_____	palliate	_____

A. Choose a word from your spelling list that fits each definition below. Find the word in the word search and highlight it.

H	E	T	A	N	I	M	R	E	T	E	D	N	I	E
A	I	M	P	O	R	T	U	N	A	T	E	N	P	T
S	U	B	J	U	G	A	T	E	C	A	D	E	S	A
S	W	L	J	P	R	O	P	I	T	I	A	T	E	G
C	O	O	Z	R	Z	H	G	N	S	T	H	A	T	I
I	E	M	Y	E	P	B	M	C	E	N	P	G	A	T
N	T	T	N	V	R	V	R	H	T	A	E	R	C	S
T	A	F	A	O	I	K	O	A	T	R	U	I	N
I	I	I	P	R	M	L	V	A	C	S	P	P	R	I
L	V	S	V	I	U	B	D	T	A	B	E	X	T	V
L	B	T	N	C	L	D	U	E	L	U	T	E	X	R
A	O	A	N	A	G	D	B	L	P	S	U	K	E	R
T	T	F	I	T	A	W	G	O	A	D	A	N	E	F
E	T	A	R	E	T	E	V	N	I	T	T	J	P	S
Y	E	T	A	R	E	N	O	X	E	R	E	U	T	U

1. declare free from blame _____

2. bring into submission, vanquish _____

3. having a long established habit or activity that is unlikely to change _____

4. just begun and therefor not fully formed or developed _____

5. make less angry or hostile _____

6. remove from text matter thought to be unsuitable _____

7. provide evidence to support or prove the truth of _____

8. bring about or initiate _____

9. promote or make widely known _____

10. free from a constraint or difficulty _____

11. avoid or prevent something undesirable _____

12. persistent, especially to the point of annoyance _____

13. win or regain favour of (especially the gods) by doing something for them _____

14. speak or act in an evasive way _____

You will also find: extricate, indeterminate, indiscriminate, perpetuate, scintillate, somnambulate.

Unit 14: hy-, -sion

Look up the meaning and then learn these words.

hybrid	hydrate	hydraulic	hydrofoil
hydrology	hydroponics	hyena	hygiene
hyperbole	hyperthermia	hyphen	hypodermis
hypotension	hypothesis	hypoxia	hysteria
aspersion	aversion	condescension	derision
digression	dispersion	effusion	egression
expulsion	impression	interspersion	precision
preclusion	repercussion	secession	suasion

Etymology or Word Origin— aversion

Aversion comes from the Latin *aversionem* from past participle stem of *aversus* "turned away, backwards, behind, hostile." In the 1590s it was used in the literal sense of "a turning away from."

The prefixes hydro- means having to do with water, e.g., hydrodynamic.

A. In the space below write three spelling words that contain the prefix hydro-.

1. _____	2. _____	3. _____

The prefix hypo– means under, below, slightly, e.g., hypocotyl, hypothermia.

B. In the space below write the spelling words that contain the prefix hypo-.

1. _____	2. _____	3. _____

The prefix hyper– means over, usually implying excess or exaggeration, e.g., hypertension.

C. In the space below write the spelling words that contains this prefix. Use your dictionary to find another word with this prefix.

1. _____	2. _____	3. _____

D. Write the adjectival form of the following nouns.

1. expulsion _____	2. secession _____
3. hysteria _____	4. dispersion _____
5. hygiene _____	6. impression _____

A. Find a word starting with hy– from your spelling list to fit the following definitions.

1. hy_____   combine chemically with water

2. hy_____   the layer of cells immediately below the dermis of a plant

3. hy_____   used to indicate the division of a word

4. hy_____   a proposed explanation made on the basis of limited evidence as a starting point for further investigation

5. hy_____   exaggerated statements not meant to be taken literally

6. hy_____   the process of growing plants in sand, stones or liquid with added nutrients

7. hy_____   the science of the properties and movement of earth's water

8. hy_____   a deficiency in the amount of oxygen reaching tissues

9. hy_____   a dog-like African mammal

10. hy_____   wild, uncontrollable excitement or laughter

11. hy_____   the offspring of two plants or animals of different species or varieties

12. hy_____   denoting or relating to a liquid moving in a confined space under pressure

B. Write the definition of the following spelling words.

1. digression: _____

_____

2. effusion: _____

3. preclusion: _____

_____

4. derision: _____

Unit 15: Revision

Revise these words.

actuate	aspersion	condescension	conspiratorial
contraindicate	delineate	deferential	denigrate
effusion	enervate	expiate	expurgate
hydrology	hypothesis	hypoxia	inchoate
inconsequential	obdurate	obviate	precedential
promulgate	proprietorial	quintessential	vacillate

A. Complete the following:

1. The prefixes in-, im-, il– or ir– mean _____

2. The prefixes dis– and dif- mean _____

   _____

3. The prefix ex– means _____

4. The prefix hyper– means _____

5. The prefix pro– means _____

6. The prefixes hydro– means _____

7. The prefix con– or com- can mean _____

8. Con-, com– col- or coll- can also mean _____

9. The prefix hypo– means _____

10. The prefix pre– means _____ and the prefix pro- means ____

    _____

11. Homonyms are _____

    _____

B. Use a word from your spelling list to complete each sentence below.

1. The offer on the house will _____ the need of an auction.

2. John _____ between flying or cruising to New Zealand. (past tense)

A. Solve the crossword puzzle using words from your spelling list.

Across

1. branch of science concerned with the properties of earth's water
3. an attack on the reputation of someone or something
4. make someone act in particular way
6. one who has legal title to something, owner
7. relating to a previous case or legal decision
8. describe or portray
9. criticise unfairly, disparage

Down

1. <u>adjectival form</u> of proposed explanation based on limited investigation as basis for scientific investigation
2. showing respect, obsequious
5. put law into effect by official proclamation

B. Divide the following words into syllables. Explain the word meaning to an adult. (Being able to divide a word will help with spelling it.)

1. quintessential _____   2. expurgate _____

© Valerie Marett
Coroneos Publications

Australian Homeschooling #569
Successful Spelling 8

Unit 16: -eous

Look up the meaning and then learn these words.

advantageous	aqueous	consanguineous
contemporaneous	courageous	crustaceous
discourteous	erroneous	extemporaneous
extraneous	herbaceous	heterogeneous
instantaneous	nauseous	predaceous
simultaneous	spontaneous	vitreous

Etymology or Word Origin—erroneous

Erroneous comes from the Latin *erroneus* "vagrant, wandering", from *erronem,* "a wanderer, vagabond," and from past participle stem of *errare* "to wander; to err". About 1300 it was used in Old French *errer* to mean "go astray, lose one's way; make a mistake."

A. Write the modern definition of erroneous in the space provided below.

_____

B. Write two words from your spelling list that relate to water or living in water.

1. _____   2. _____

C. Write the two synonyms in your spelling list mean "immediately."

1. _____   2. _____

D. When the word ends in "ge", e.g., outrage, **there is a small group of adjectives that take the ending -eous to keep the "g that says j,"** e.g., outrageous. **This applies to two words in your spelling list. Write them below.**

1. _____   2. _____

E. Use each word below in a sentence.

1. herbaceous: _____

_____

2. extemporaneous: _____

_____

3. predaceous: _____

_____

A. Find a word from the spelling list that fits each definition.

1. existing at or occurring at the same period of time _____

2. like glass in appearance or physical properties _____

3. descended from the same ancestor _____

4. spoken or done without preparation _____

5. diverse in character; varied in content _____

6. living by or preying on animals _____

7. incorrect, wrong _____

8. containing or like water _____

9. showing rudeness towards others _____

10. feeling inclined to vomit _____

11. having an open, natural and uninhibited manner _____

12. favourable circumstances that increase the chances of success _____

B. Use a dictionary to change the words below to nouns.

1. spontaneous_____   2. advantageous _____

3. instantaneous _____   4. discourteous _____

5. contemporaneous _____ 6. predacious _____

7. extraneous _____   8. erroneous _____

C. Write two antonyms for each word below. Do not just add a prefix to the word.

1. courageous _____   _____

2. discourteous _____   _____

3. erroneous _____   _____

4. advantageous _____   _____

5. extemporaneous _____

Unit 17: -cious

Look up the meaning and then learn these words.

audacious	auspicious	avaricious	capricious
fallacious	loquacious	luscious	malicious
mendacious	officious	perspicacious	pernicious
pertinacious	precocious	pugnacious	rapacious
unsuspicious	tenacious	vivacious	voracious

Etymology or Word Origin—pernicious

Pernicious comes from the Latin *perniciosus* "destructive;" from *pernicies* "destruction, death, ruin;" from *per-* "completely" + *necis* "violent death, murder;" It is related to *necare* "to kill," *nocere* "to hurt, injure, harm," *noxa* "harm, injury."

<u>**The prefix per– means through or intensive,**</u> e.g., persecute, persuade.

A. In the space below write the spelling words that contain the prefix per-.

1. _____	2. _____	3. _____

<u>**The prefix un– means not, against, opposite,**</u> e.g., unequal, unceasing.

B. In the space below write the spelling word that contains the prefix un-. Write 2 more words with this prefix. Do not use the examples above.

1. _____	2. _____	3. _____

<u>**The prefix mal- means bad or badly,**</u> e.g., malformation, malfunction.

C. In the space below write the spelling word that contains the prefix mal-. Write the definition of the word beside it.

_____   _____

D. Write the most common form of the noun and adverb of each adjective below.

adjective	noun	adverb
1. avaricious	_____	_____
2. tenacious	_____	_____
3. pertinacious	_____	_____
4. mendacious	_____	_____

A. Write the definition of each word below.

1. avaricious:_____
   _____

2. fallacious: _____

3. rapacious: _____

4. officious: _____
   _____

5. auspicious: _____
   _____

B. Choose a spelling word to fit each definition.

1. wanting or devouring great quantities of food; engaging in an activity with great eagerness   _____

2. holding firmly to an opinion or course of action   _____

3. tending to talk a great deal   _____

4. given to unaccountable changes of mood or behaviour; unpredictable   _____

5. having developed at an earlier age than expected   _____

6. attractive, lively, animated, (especially of a woman)   _____

7. having a rich taste; appealing to the senses; pleasingly rich   _____

8. not telling the truth, lying   _____

9. having a ready insight and understanding of things   _____

10. showing a willingness to take surprisingly bold risks; showing an impudent lack of respect   _____

11. malevolent; intending to cause harm   _____

12. tending to keep a firm hold of something; not readily relinquishing a position; persistent   _____

13. having a harmful effect, especially in a gradual way   _____

Unit 18: -ious

Look up the meaning and then learn these words.

acrimonious	atrocious	conscientious	contentious
copious	deleterious	disputatious	dubious
egregious	fastidious	fractious	gregarious
harmonious	ignominious	impecunious	impervious
insidious	licentious	litigious	multifarious

The suffix -ious forms adjectives charecterised by, full of, e.g., copious means <u>full of</u> ideas or speech.

Etymology or Word Origin—egregious

Egregious comes from the Latin *egregius* "distinguished, excellent, extraordinary," and from the phrase *ex grege* "rising above the flock". About 1530s the meaning "distinguished, eminent, excellent" started to be used. The meaning "oustandingly bad," which is now predominant, arose in the late 16th century.

The prefix co– means with, together, e.g., cooperate.

A. In the space below write the spelling word that contains the prefix co-. Write 2 more words with this prefix. Do not use the example above.

1. _____ 2. _____ 3. _____

B. You have already learnt the meaning of the prefix im– and in-. Write the meaning below. Write 3 words from your spelling list that contain these prefixes.

The prefix im– and in– mean _____

1. _____ 2. _____ 3. _____

C. Divide the following words into syllables.

1. acrimonious _____ 2. ignominious _____

3. gregarious _____ 4. impecunious _____

5. deleterious _____ 6. multifarious _____

7. copious _____ 8. litigious _____

D. Write a sentence using one of your spelling words.

_____

Choose a word from your spelling list that fits each definition below. Some words have more than one meaning. Find the word in the word search and highlight it.

C	D	U	C	V	T	F	R	A	C	T	I	O	U	S
O	D	S	S	U	O	I	P	O	C	W	D	S	S	U
N	A	M	U	L	T	I	F	A	R	I	O	U	S	O
S	C	H	O	O	C	M	Z	Y	S	L	O	O	U	I
C	R	A	I	B	I	D	O	P	I	I	K	I	O	M
I	I	R	D	F	U	G	U	C	C	X	M	R	I	O
E	M	M	I	A	M	T	E	O	A	P	B	E	V	N
N	O	O	S	S	A	N	R	R	E	S	X	T	R	G
T	N	N	N	T	T	T	Q	C	G	B	C	E	E	I
I	I	I	I	I	A	O	U	M	S	E	W	L	P	K
O	O	O	O	D	D	N	X	H	S	U	F	E	M	I
U	U	U	E	I	I	Y	K	Q	Q	H	G	D	I	U
S	S	S	U	O	I	T	N	E	T	N	O	C	R	C
X	K	W	U	U	L	I	T	I	G	I	O	U	S	Y
S	E	S	K	S	U	O	I	R	A	G	E	R	G	M

1. fond of having heated arguments _____

2. in a thorough and responsible way _____

3. fond of company, sociable _____

4. angry and bitter _____

5. very attentive to and very concerned about accuracy and detail _____

6. having little or no money _____

7. having many varied parts or aspects _____

8. causing or likely to cause an argument, giving to provoking argument _____

9. proceeding in a gradual, subtle way, but with harmful effects _____

10. outstandingly bad or shocking _____

11. not allowing fluid to pass through _____

12. horrifyingly wicked; extremely bad or unpleasant _____

13. disregarding accepted conventions, especially in grammar or literary style _____

Others words in the puzzle: copious, harmonious, deleterious, fractious, litigious.

Unit 19: more -ious, -oe says ee

Look up the meaning and then learn these words.

meritorious	nefarious	noxious	oblivious
obnoxious	obsequious	parsimonious	penurious
precarious	prodigious	punctilious	repetitious
sacrilegious	salubrious	sanctimonious	spurious
supercilious	surreptitious	temerarious	vicarious
amoeba	onomatopoeia	pharmacopoeia	subpoena

Etymology or Word Origin—surreptitious
Surreptitious comes from the Latin *surrepticius* "stolen, furtive, clandestine," from *surreptus*, past participle of *surripere,* "seize secretly, take away, steal, plagiarize."

The prefix sacr-, sanc- or secre- means sacred, e.g. sacrosanct, desecrate.

A. In the space below write the spelling word that contains the prefix sacr-. Write 2 more words with this prefix. Do not use the example above.

> 1. _____   2. _____   3. _____

The prefix pre- and pur- mean before, e.g., precede.

The prefix pro- means for or forward, e.g., propel.

B. In the space below write the spelling word that contains the prefix pre- and pro-.

> 1. _____   2. _____

The prefix super- means above, beyond, to a great or extreme degree or of a higher kind, e.g., superior, superimpose.

C. In the space below write the spelling word that contains the prefix super-. Write the definition of the word.

> _____ : _____

D. Change the following adjectives to adverbs.

1. obsequious _____	2. surreptitious _____
3. repetitious _____	4. supercilious _____
5. obnoxious _____	6. precarious _____

A. Use the following words in sentences to show you understand their meaning.

1. meritorious: _____

   _____

2. oblivious: _____

   _____

3. pharmacopoeia: _____

   _____

4. spurious: _____

   _____

B. Find a spelling word that fits each definition.

1. reckless, rash   _____

2. a single celled animal   _____

3. poverty stricken, very poor; unwilling to
   spend money   _____

4. deserving reward or praise; likely to succeed
   on merits of the case   _____

5. living through the actions or feelings of another person_____

6. not being what it purports to be; false   _____

7. extremely unpleasant   _____

8. a writ ordering a person to attend court   _____

9. criminal, wickedly evil, malicious   _____

10. making a show of being morally superior to others   _____

11. healthy; generally favourable to the mind
    and body   _____

12. not securely held or in position; dependent on
    chance, uncertain   _____

13. poisonous or very unpleasant   _____

14. remarkably great in extent or size; abnormal   _____

Unit 20: Revision

Revise these words.

acrimonious	avaricious	capricious	conscientious
contemporaneous	contentious	discourteous	extraneous
fastidious	ignominious	instantaneous	litigious
luscious	nauseous	noxious	obsequious
pernicious	pertinacious	predaceous	prodigious
subpoena	surreptitious	tenacious	vivacious

A. Complete the meaning of the following prefixes:

1. un– means _____

2. pre– and pur– mean _____

3. per– means _____

4. co– means _____

5. sacr– means _____

6. mal– means _____

7. pro– means _____

8. super– means _____

B. Write sentences for each word below showing you understand their meaning.

1. vivacious: _____
    _____

2. obsequious: _____
    _____

3. capricious: _____
    _____

4. noxious: _____
    _____

5. luscious: _____
    _____

Solve the crossword puzzle using words from your spelling list.

Across

2. a writ ordering a person to attend court
5. not readily relinquishing a position
6. existing at or occurring at the same period of time
7. deserving or causing public disgrace or shame
8. occurring or done instantly
9. kept secret, especially as it would not be approved of

Down

1. causing or likely to cause an argument
3. angry and bitter (discussion)
4. wishing to do one's work or duty thoroughly

B. Change these adjectives by completing the chart below.

Adjective	Noun	Adverb
1. avaricious	_____	_____
2. extraneous	_____	_____
3. discourteous	_____	_____

Unit 21: -ent, -ment

Look up the meaning and then learn these words.

abhorrent	ambivalent	augment	belligerent
coherent	constituent	decadent	denouncement
deterrent	ebullient	effervescent	embezzlement
evanescent	exigent	expedient	fraudulent
impertinent	incumbent	insurgent	intransigent

Etymology or Word Origin—abhorrent

Abhorrent comes from the Latin *abhorentem* meaning "incongruous, inappropriate," and from the present participle of *abhorrere* "shrink back from, be remote from, be out of harmony with."

The suffixes -ent or -ant appear in nouns and adjectives of Latin meaning.

The prefix ex– means out of, away from, lacking, former, e.g., external, extraordinary.

A. In the space below write the spelling words that contain the prefix ex-.

1. _____ 2. _____

The prefix ambi- means both ways, e.g., ambidextrous.

B. In the space below write the spelling word that contains the prefix ambi-. Write 2 more words with this prefix. Do not use the example above.

1. _____ 2. _____ 3. _____

The prefixes ab- or abs- means away from, off, e.g., abrupt, absolve.

C. In the spaces below write the spelling word that contains the prefix ab-. Write 2 more words with this prefix. Do not use the example above.

1. _____ 2. _____ 3. _____

D. Write the following words in sentences to show you understand their meaning:

1. expedient: _____

_____

2. belligerent: _____

_____

A. Draw a line from the definition to the correct spelling word.

1.	a person fighting against a government or invading force	a.	ebullient
2.	logical, consistent, forming a unified whole	b.	intransigent
3.	cheerful and full of energy	c.	decadent
4.	make greater by adding to it, increase	d.	embezzlement
5.	not showing proper respect, rude	e.	insurgent
6.	having mixed feelings or contradictory ideas about something	f.	impertinent
7.	an action that is cheating or dishonest gains from that action	g.	abhorrent
8.	unwilling to change one's views or agree	h.	evanescent
9.	repugnant, inspiring disgust and loathing	i.	coherent
10.	necessary as a duty or responsibility, a person holding office	j.	deterrent
11.	pressing, demanding, requiring immediate action	k.	augment
12.	a person who is luxuriously self-indulgent	l.	exigent
13.	a thing that discourages a person from doing something	m.	ambivalent
14.	soon passing out of sight or memory or existence	n.	incumbent
15.	theft or misappropriation of funds placed in your trust	o.	fraudulent

B. Use a dictionary to complete the chart.

	Noun	Adjective	Verb
1.	_____	abhorrent	_____
2.	denouncement		_____
3.	_____	constituent	_____
4.	_____	effervescent	_____

Unit 22: more -ent, -ence

Look up the meaning and then learn these words.

malevolent	munificent	negligent	obsolescent
precedent	prurient	reminiscent	truculent
acquiescence	ambience	belligerence	complacence
concurrence	credence	divergence	eloquence
indolence	nascence	opalescence	precedence
resplendence	reticence	somnolence	turbulence

Etymology or Word Origin—malevolent

Malevolent comes from the Latin *malevolentem* meaning "ill-disposed, spiteful, envious."

The prefix re- means back or again, e.g., realign, revise.

A. In the space below write the spelling words that contain the prefix re-.

1. _____   2. _____

The prefixes ob-, oc-, of-, op- mean towards, against, in the way, e.g., obtain, oppose.

B. In the space below write the spelling word that contains the prefix ob- or op-. Write 1 more word using either prefix. Do not use the example above.

1. _____   2. _____   3. _____

The prefix di- or dy- means two, twice, double, e.g., divide.

C. In the space below write the spelling word that contain the prefix di–. Write 2 more words using either prefix. Do not use the example above.

1. _____   2. _____   3. _____

D. Divide each word below into syllables.

1. munificent	_____	2. credence	_____
3. prurient	_____	4. acquiescence	_____
5. nascence	_____	6. turbulence	_____
7. belligerence	_____	8. reminiscent	_____

A. Find a spelling word that fits each definition.

1. the process or state of dividing or separating _____

2. the reluctant acceptance of something without protest _____

3. being born, starting to grow or develop _____

4. arousing an immoderate or unwholesome or desire _____

5. having or showing a wish to do evil to others _____

6. reserved, not speaking freely _____

7. the character or atmosphere of a place _____

8. the condition of no longer being used or useful _____

9. eager or quick to fight, aggressively defiant _____

10. fluent or persuasive speaking or writing _____

11. an early event or action that is regarded as an example _____

12. the simultaneous occurrence of events or circumstances _____

13. the quality of almost unbelievable beauty or majesty _____

14. suggesting something by its resemblance _____

15. avoidance of activity or exertion; laziness _____

B. Look up the difference between <u>precedent</u> and <u>precedence</u> and <u>obsolescent</u> and <u>opalescence.</u> Explain them to an adult.

C. Write the adjectival and adverbial form of each word below.

	adjective	adverb
1. turbulence	_____	_____
2. somnolence	_____	_____
3. belligerence	_____	_____

Unit 23: -ance

Look up the meaning and then learn these words. –ance or –ence are suffixes of nouns showing state, quality, action or process.

aberrance	abeyance	acquaintance	assurance
cognizance	dissonance	emittance	encumbrance
exorbitance	exuberance	flamboyance	forbearance
malfeasance	nuance	obeisance	preponderance
protuberance	pursuance	recalcitrance	reconnaissance

Etymology or Word Origin—malfeasance

Malfeasance comes from Latin *facere* "to do," from Latin *maleficentia* "evildoing, mischievousness, injury," 1690s, from French *malfaisance* "wrongdoing." Originally spelt as maleficence but now replaced by malfeasance.

The prefix ab- or abs- means away from, off, e.g., absolve, abrupt.

A. In the space below write the spelling words that contains the prefix ab-. Write 1 other words containing this prefix.

1. _____   2. _____   3. _____

The prefix for- or fore- means before, e.g., forecast, fortune.

B. In the space below write the spelling word that contains the prefix for-. Write 2 other words containing this prefix. Do not use the examples above.

1. _____   2. _____   3. _____

The prefix re- means back or again, e.g., report, realign, retract.

C. In the space below write the two spelling words that contain the prefix re-. Write 1 other word containing this prefix.

1. _____   2. _____   3. _____

D. Write an antonym for each of the following words.

1. exorbitance _____   2. flamboyance _____

3. preponderance_____   4. acquaintance _____

5. recalcitrance_____   6. exuberance _____

7. assurance _____   8. cognizance _____

A. Choose a word from your spelling list that fits each definition below. Find the word in the word search and highlight it.

R	E	C	O	N	N	A	I	S	S	A	N	C	E	E
W	E	C	N	A	R	E	D	N	O	P	E	R	P	C
B	X	G	N	U	A	N	C	E	I	R	N	A	H	N
E	O	R	L	A	N	N	D	R	C	O	C	B	D	A
C	R	E	N	R	R	B	G	R	T	T	U	E	J	R
N	B	C	H	K	N	T	M	I	M	U	M	R	A	E
A	I	N	I	N	V	X	I	U	C	B	B	R	D	B
R	T	A	M	B	I	A	N	C	E	E	R	A	Z	U
A	A	S	H	L	K	Q	M	O	L	R	A	N	X	X
E	N	A	C	Q	U	A	I	N	T	A	N	C	E	E
B	C	E	C	O	G	N	I	Z	A	N	C	E	F	S
R	E	F	P	U	R	S	U	A	N	C	E	E	S	E
O	A	L	Y	E	C	N	A	S	I	E	B	O	R	J
F	L	A	M	B	O	Y	A	N	C	E	M	C	M	O
C	V	M	E	C	N	A	N	O	S	S	I	D	F	U

1. survey of an area, especially a military examination to locate an enemy _____

2. deviating from the usual course _____

3. knowledge or awareness, perception _____

4. grossly excessive price demanded _____

5. obstinately unco-operative, objecting to constraints _____

6. a person one knows slightly _____

7. evildoing, injury _____

8. subtle difference in shade of meaning, feeling colour etc. _____

9. prominent, sticking out _____

10. the quality of being full of cheerfulness, energy or excitement _____

11. the quality of being bright, colourful and very noticeable _____

Other words found in the crossword: preponderance, forbearance, encumbrance, pursuance, obeisance, ambiance, dissonance.

Unit 24: -ous

Look up the meaning and then learn these words.

abstentious	ambiguous	anomalous	assiduous
cantankerous	clamorous	congruous	conspicuous
contemptuous	contiguous	credulous	disadvantageous
fatuous	garrulous	gratuitous	heinous
horrendous	indigenous	ingenuous	incongruous
innocuous	magnanimous	meticulous	monogamous

-ous makes an adjective from a noun and means having, full of, having to do with, inclined to.

Etymology or Word Origin—meticulous

Meticulous comes from the Latin *meticulosus* "fearful, timid," literally "full of fear," from *metus* "fear, dread, apprehension, anxiety." Sense of "fussy about details" is first recorded in English 1827.

The prefixes con-, co-, cog-,coll- com- and cor- mean with, together, e.g., converse, cognate, collaborate, compress, correct.

A. In the space below write the spelling words that contain the prefix con-.

1. _____   2. _____

3. _____   4. _____

The prefixes in-,im-, il-, ir- mean not, e.g., innocuous, impossible, illegible, irresolute. **The prefixes in-, im– can also mean into, on, near, towards,** e.g., instead, import.

B. In the space below write the spelling words that contain the prefix in-.

1. _____   2. _____

3. _____   4. _____

The prefix magn- means great, e.g., magnify, magnificent.

The prefix mono- means one, e.g., monologue.

C. In the space below write the spelling words that contain the prefixes magn– and mono-

1. _____   2. _____

Use one of the two words above in a sentence.

_____

A. Write a noun formed from each word below.

1. abstentious _____
2. meticulous _____
3. contemptuous _____
4. magnanimous _____
5. heinous _____
6. ingenuous _____
7. garrulous _____
8. conspicuous _____
9. horrendous _____
10. anomalous _____

N.B. While "ness" is sometimes added when an adjective is changed to a noun, it is not added to a verb to make a noun. While the word "wellness" has been accepted into our language it is grammatically incorrect as "well" is an adverb not an adjective.

B. Write an antonym for each word below.

1. ambiguous _____
2. contiguous _____
3. innocuous _____
4. disadvantageous _____
5. clamorous _____
6. conspicuous _____
7. fatuous _____
8. gratuitous _____
9. contemptuous _____
10. cantankerous _____

C. Find a spelling word that fits each definition.

1. silly, pointless _____

2. not in harmony or keeping with the surroundings _____

3. having an irregular or deviant feature _____

4. scornful, insolent _____

5. being married to one person at a time _____

6. utterly odious or wicked _____

7. talkative, especially on trivial matters, loquacious _____

8. making a loud and confused noise _____

9. gullible, too ready to believe _____

Unit 25: Revision

Revise these words.

aberrance	abhorrent	acquiescence	belligerent
clamorous	credence	dissonance	divergence
embezzlement	encumbrance	exuberance	forbearance
gratuitous	impertinent	incumbent	innocuous
magnanimous	malfeasance	nuance	precedence
preponderance	recalcitrance	reminiscent	reticence

A. Complete the meaning of the following prefixes:

1. The prefix re- means _____.

2. The prefix di- or dy- means _____.

3. The prefixes ab- or abs- means _____.

4. The prefix am- or ami- means _____.

5. The prefixes con-, co-, cog-,coll- com- and cor- mean _____.

6. The prefix mono– means _____.

7. The prefix ambi- means _____.

8. The prefixes ab- or abs- means _____.

9. The prefix ex- means _____.

10. The prefixes ob-, oc-, of, op- mean _____.

11. The prefixes in-,im-, il-, ir- mean _____. The prefixes in-, im– can

   also mean _____.

12. The prefix magn– means _____.

13. The prefix for- or fore- means _____.

B. Write antonyms for each word below.

1. belligerent _____   2. magnanimous _____

A. Solve the crossword puzzle using words from your spelling list.

Across

1. priority in time, order or rank
4. belief in or acceptance of something as true
6. patient endurance, refraining
7. the quality or fact of being greater in number
8. a subtle distinction or variation **of** meaning, expression or sound
9. very enthusiastic, high-spirited
10. to appropriate funds fraudulently to ones own use

Down

2. mortgage or charge on a property
3. having an obstinate uncooperative attitude
5. departing from an accepted standard

B. Write a sentence using each word shown below.

1. abhorrent: _____

_____

2. incumbent: _____

_____

Unit 26: more -ous

Look up the meaning and then learn these words.

obstreperous	onerous	piteous	platitudinous
posthumous	precipitous	preposterous	presumptuous
querulous	raucous	scrupulous	scurrilous
slanderous	solicitous	superfluous	tempestuous
ubiquitous	unanimous	unctuous	vociferous

Etymology or Word Origin—vociferous

Vociferous comes from the Latin *vociferari* "to shout, yell, cry out;" from *vox* "voice" + stem of *ferre* "to carry."

The prefix sol- means alone, e.g., solo.

A. In the space below write the spelling word that contain the prefix sol-. Write a word of your own that contains the same prefix.

1. _____   2. _____

The prefix pre- and pur- mean before, e.g., prefix.

B. In the space below write the spelling words that contains the prefix pre-.

1. _____   2. _____   3. _____

C. Pronounciation is very important. Two of your spelling words have the long u sound. Write these words below.

1. _____   2. _____

D. Divide each spelling word below into syllables.

1.	obstreperous	_____	2. presumptuous	_____
3.	querulous	_____	4. unanimous	_____
5.	scrupulous	_____	6. posthumous	_____
7.	platitudinous	_____	8. raucous	_____

E. Choose a word from your list and write a sentence showing you understand its meaning.

_____

A.   Find a spelling word that fits each definition.

1. involving a great deal of effort, trouble or difficulty _____

2. failing to observe the limits of what is permitted or appropriate _____

3. false and malicious spoken statement _____

4. appearing or found everywhere _____

5. contrary to reason or common sense, absurd _____

6. making or spreading scandalous claims about someone _____

7. remark or statement used too often to be interesting or thoughtful _____

8. unnecessary as there is already enough _____

9. noisy and difficult to control _____

10. excessively flattering or ingratiating _____

11. expressing or characterised by vehement opinions _____

12. complaining in a petulant or whining manner _____

13. careful, thorough, extremely attentive to detail _____

14. making a disturbing or harsh noise _____

15. awarded or appearing after the death of the originator _____

16. showing interest or concern _____

17. all in agreement, meeting where motion is carried by everyone involved _____

18. contrary to reason or common sense, utterly absurd _____

19. characterised by strong and turbulent emotions _____

20. dangerously high or steep, done quickly without thought _____

Unit 27: -ise, -ize, –al

Look up the meaning and then learn these words.

aggrandize	categorise	conceptualise	enfranchise
galvanise	ostracise	plagiarise	scrutinize
accrual	actuarial	alluvial	diabolical
effectual	egotistical	empirical	ethereal
farcical	inimical	jurisdictional	peripheral
paradoxical	prejudicial	rebuttal	uncontroversial

Etymology or Word Origin—inimical

Inimical comes from the Latin *inimicalis* "hostile," and from the Latin *inimicus* "unfriendly; an enemy".

A. Divide each spelling word below into syllables.

1. alluvial _____
2. plagiarise _____
3. egotistical _____
4. uncontroversial _____
5. paradoxical _____
6. diabolical _____
7. farcical _____
7. ethereal _____

B. Change the following verbs to nouns.

1. enfranchise _____
2. scrutinize _____
3. categorise _____
4. plagiarize _____
5. conceptualise _____
6. aggrandize _____

C. Change the following into adverbs.

1. egotistical _____
2. etherial _____
3. inimical _____
4. empirical _____
5. diabolical _____
6. prejudicial _____
7. effectual _____
8. potential _____

D. Write a sentence using one of your spelling words.

_____

Find a spelling word that fits each definition.

1. disgracefully bad or unpleasant _____

2. increase the power, status or wealth of _____

3. tending to obstruct or harm _____

4. resembling a farce because of its absurd
   and ridiculous aspects _____

5. seemingly absurd or self-contradictory _____

6. take the idea or work of someone else
   and pass it off as your own _____

7. give the right to vote _____

8. extremely delicate and light in a way that
   seems not of this world _____

9. exclude from a society or group _____

10. the adding together of interest or
    investments over a period of time _____

11. based on or concerned with verifiable
    evidence or experience rather than theory _____

12. relating to the work of compiling and
    analysing statistics to calculate insurance
    risks and premiums _____

13. extremely light, delicate, heavenly or spiritual _____

14. an instance of a claim to prove that
    evidence given by a witness is false _____

15. examine and inspect closely and thoroughly _____

16. soil, sand, silt, clay, gravel or other matter
    deposited by flood water _____

17. relating to the official power to make legal
    decisions and judgements _____

18. place in a particular class or group _____

19. form a concept or idea of something _____

© Valerie Marett
Coroneos Publications

Australian Homeschooling #569
Successful Spelling 8

Unit 28: -ic

Look up the meaning and then learn these words.

acerbic	aeronautic	aesthetic	altruistic
antagonistic	ascetic	bureaucratic	caricature
cathartic	didactic	eclectic	enigmatic
esoteric	laconic	lethargic	linguistic
mnemonic	pragmatic	rhetoric	vitriolic

Etymology or Word Origin—didactic

Didactic comes from the Greek *didaktikos* "apt at teaching," from *didaktos* "taught."

The prefixes acer-, acid-, acri- mean bitter, sour, sharp, e.g., acerbity, acidity, acrimony.

A. Write the list word that has a prefix acer-. Write a sentence using the word to show you understand its meaning.

_____ : _____

_____

The prefixes aero- or aer- mean air, of air craft, e.g., aerial.

B. Write the list word that has a prefix aero-. Write two other words with the prefix aer- or aero-. Do not use the example shown above.

1. _____   2. _____   3. _____

C. Write the answer to each question below:

1. noun form of the adjective <u>aeronautic</u>   _____

2. noun form of the adjective <u>lethargic</u>   _____

3. noun form of the adjective <u>antagonistic</u>   _____

4. noun form of the adjective <u>aesthetic</u>   _____

5. noun form of the adjective <u>enigmatic</u>   _____

6. adverbial form of the adjective <u>laconic</u>   _____

7. noun form of the adjective <u>antagonistic</u>   _____

Choose a word from your spelling list that fits each definition below. Some words have more than one meaning. Find the word in the word search and highlight it.

C	H	A	R	A	C	T	E	R	I	S	T	I	C	C
C	C	E	N	L	I	N	G	U	I	S	T	I	C	I
I	I	S	G	T	T	D	Z	M	I	Z	T	N	I	N
T	G	T	Y	K	A	J	F	H	A	U	P	Q	N	O
C	R	H	S	M	R	G	H	D	A	B	F	V	O	C
A	A	E	H	I	C	N	O	N	E	C	C	I	M	A
D	H	T	R	F	U	I	O	N	N	B	X	T	E	L
I	T	I	H	V	A	R	T	H	I	P	M	R	N	Q
D	E	C	E	A	E	S	T	A	G	S	R	O	M	O
R	L	I	T	A	R	H	C	L	M	F	T	L	L	A
N	I	B	O	K	U	T	U	E	A	G	V	I	Y	I
H	M	R	R	M	B	W	I	T	T	X	A	C	C	T
B	N	E	I	J	T	N	R	C	I	I	D	R	R	Y
S	U	C	C	I	T	C	E	L	C	E	C	H	P	I
P	O	A	E	S	T	O	R	I	C	Q	W	S	H	A

1. a feature or quality belonging to a person place or thing _____

2. showing a self-less concern for the wellbeing of others _____

3. deriving ideas, style or taste from a broad and diverse range of sources _____

4. showing or feeling hostility towards someone _____

5. relating to a system of government in which most of the important decisions are taken by officials _____

6. in the manner of a teacher, particularly as to appear patronising _____

7. difficult to interpret or understand _____

8. concerned with beauty or appreciation of beauty _____

9. sluggish and apathetic _____

10. tasting sour or bitter, sharp and forthright comment_____

Other words hidden in word search: aeronautic, acerbic, ascetic, cathartic, laconic, linguistic, mnemonic, pragmatic

Australian Homeschooling #569
Successful Spelling 8

Unit 29: -ible, -able

Look up the meaning and then learn these words.

contemptible	discernible	feasible	gullible
incontrovertible	incorrigible	inexhaustible	irascible
ostensible	reprehensible	submersible	susceptible
despicable	execrable	impeccable	ineffable
inexorable	inimitable	palpable	redoubtable

The suffixes –ible and –able are commonly used to terminate adjectives and generally add a notion of capable of; allowed; worthy of.

Etymology or Word Origin—feasible
Feasible comes from the Anglo-French *faisible*, and from Old French *faisable* meaning "possible, that may be done; easy, convenient."

A. Revision: Write the meaning of each suffix below. Write a word from the spelling list that contains this suffix.

1. con-: _____ 2. in-: _____

3. dis-: _____

4. ex-: _____

5. im-: _____ 6. re-: _____

B. Write an antonym for each word below.

1. inexhaustible _____ 2. palpable _____

3. discernible _____ 4. impeccable _____

5. despicable _____ 6. gullible _____

C. Write an synonym for each word below.

1. incorrigible _____ 2. susceptible _____

3. execrable _____ 4. despicable _____

5. ostensible _____ 6. contemptible _____

7. feasible _____ 8. redoubtable _____

9. incontrovertible _____ 10. ineffable _____

A. Write the definition of each word below.

1. discernible: _____

2. inimitable: _____

3. irascible: _____

4. ineffable: _____

5. submersible: _____

6. reprehensible: _____

B. Find a spelling word that fits each definition.

1. formidable, especially as an opponent _____

2. impossible to stop or prevent _____

3. easily persuaded to do something, credulous _____

4. deserving contempt, despicable _____

5. in accordance with the highest standards _____

6. unable to be used up, in abundance _____

7. appearing to be true but not necessarily so _____

8. likely to be influenced or harmed by a particular thing _____

9. not able to be denied or disputed _____

10. not able to be changed or reformed _____

11. deserving hatred and contempt _____

12. extremely bad or unpleasant _____

C. Divide into syllables.

1. contemptible _____ 2. reprehensible _____

3. inimitable _____ 4. feasible _____

5. **Complete:** every syllable must have _____.

© Valerie Marett
Coroneos Publications

Australian Homeschooling #569
Successful Spelling 8

Unit 30: Revision

Revise these words.

acerbic	actuarial	cathartic	conceptualise
contemptible	didactic	eclectic	egotistical
farcical	gullible	impeccable	incorrigible
inexorable	irascible	obstreperous	ostracise
plagiarise	pragmatic	presumptuous	raucous
scurrilous	ubiquitous	unctuous	vitriolic

A. Complete the meaning of the following prefixes:

1. The prefixes acer-, acid-, acri- mean _____

2. The prefix sol- means _____

3. The prefix punct- means _____

4. The prefixes aero- or aer- mean _____

B. Divide each word below into syllables.

1. vitriolic _____

2. obstreperous _____

3. impeccable _____

4. presumptuous _____

5. didactic _____

6. plagarise _____

7. actuarial _____

8. scurrilous _____

C. Provide an antonym for each word below.

1. pragmatic _____

2. farcical _____

3. raucous _____

4. vitriolic _____

D. Provide a synonym for each word below.

1. ubiquitous _____

2. gullible _____

3. irascible _____

4. unctuous _____

E. Write the definition of "actuarial" below.

_____

© Valerie Marett
Coroneos Publications

Australian Homeschooling #569
Successful Spelling 8

A. Solve the crossword puzzle using words from your spelling list.

Across

1. excessively conceited or absorbed in oneself
5. making or spreading scandalous claims about someone with the intention of damaging their reputation
6. take or use another person's work or thoughts as their own
9. intended to teach, particularly as having moral instruction as the subject
10. in accordance with the highest standards
11. making a disturbingly harsh and loud sound

Down

2. not able to be changed or reformed
3. exclude from a group
4. deriving ideas, styles or tastes from a broad range of sources
7. easily persuaded to believe something, credulous
8. tasting sour or bitter

B. Use each word below in a sentence that shows you clearly understand its meaning.

1. unctuous: _____

_____

2. conceptualise: _____

_____

Unit 31: -ant, -ent,

Look up the meaning and then learn these words.

coagulant	complaisant	concomitant	desiccant
flagrant	nonchalant	penchant	petulant
poignant	repugnant	stagnant	adherent
benevolent	escarpment	exhalent	incoherent
increment	indolent	quotient	transcendent

Etymology or Word Origin—Flagrant

Flagrant comes from French in the late 15th century in the sense of 'blazing, resplendent': and from Latin *flagrant-* 'blazing', from the verb *flagrare*.

The prefixes co-, cog-, col-, coll-, com-, con-, cor- means with, together, e.g., cohesive, collaborate.

A. In the space below write the spelling words that contain the prefixes co-. com- and con-.

> 1. _____ 2. _____ 3. _____

Do you remember? The prefixes il-, im-, in- and ir- means not e.g., illegible, irresolute.

B. In the space below write the spelling words that contain the prefix in-.

> 1. _____ 2. _____ 3. _____

The prefixes pen- and pend- mean to hang, e.g., pendant, pendulum.

C. In the space below write the spelling word that contains the prefix pen-. Write two other words with the prefix pen– or pend-.Do not use the examples above.

> 1. _____ 2. _____ 3. _____

Do you remember? The prefix trans- means across, beyond, change, e.g., transform, transport.

D. In the space below write the spelling word that contains the prefix trans-. Write two other words with the prefix trans-. Do not use the examples above.

> 1. _____ 2. _____ 3. _____

E. Divide the following words into syllables.

> 1. coagulant _____ 2. transcendent _____

A. Find a spelling word that fits each definition.

1. evoking a keen sense of sadness or regret _____

2. wanting to avoid activity or excursion, lazy _____

3. willing to please others or accept what they say without protest _____

4. a strong or habitual liking for something _____

5. someone who supports a particular person, party or idea _____

6. a hygroscopic substance used as a drying agent _____

7. well meaning, kindly, serving a charitable rather than a profit making purpose _____

8. extremely distasteful _____

9. a conspicuous action considered wrong or immoral _____

10. something that naturally follows or accompanies something, naturally associated _____

11. increase or addition, especially one of a series on a fixed scale _____

12. childishly sulky or bad tempered _____

13. expressed in an incomprehensible or confusing way _____

14. a result obtained by dividing one quantity by another _____

15. a long steep slope, especially at the end of a plateau _____

B. Write a sentence showing you know the meaning of each word below.

1. coagulant: _____

_____

2. transcendent: _____

_____

3. nonchalant: _____

_____

Unit 32: more y says ee

Look up the meaning and then learn these words.

acceptability	acrimony	anonymity	apathy
arbitrary	blasphemy	brevity	criticality
epiphany	exemplary	extraordinary	frugality
gaiety	haughty	idiosyncrasy	implicitly
integrity	momentarily	notoriety	parody
parsimony	poignancy	subtlety	susceptibility

Etymology or Word Origin—consistency
Consistency comes from Medieval Latin *consistentia* or directly from Latin *consistentem.* The meaning "state of being in agreement or harmony" (with something) is from 1650s.

If "y" is the only vowel at the end of a word of more than one syllable the "y" says "ee."

A. Divide these words into syllables.

1. acceptability _____

2. blasphemy _____

3. idiosyncrasy _____

4. epiphany _____

5. poignancy _____

6. momentarily _____

7. haughty _____

8. arbitrary _____

The prefix sub- means below, secretly, e.g., substandard, subvert.

B. In the space below write the spelling word that contains the prefix sub-. Write two other words with the same prefix and meaning. (not submarine)

1. _____
2. _____
3. _____

Do you remember? The prefixes il-, im-, in- and ir-mean not, e.g. illegible, irresolute, innocuous.

C. In the space below write the spelling words that contain the prefixes im– and in-. Write a sentence using one of these words.

1. _____
2. _____

_____

_____

A. Change the following nouns into adjectives.

1. implicitly _____
2. subtlety _____
3. poignancy _____
4. frugality _____
5. subtlety _____
6. notoriety _____

B. Find a spelling word that fits each definition below.

1. the quality, state or degree of being of the highest importance _____

2. the quality of being honest and with strong moral principles _____

3. extreme unwillingness to spend money _____

4. lack of interest, enthusiasm or concern _____

5. the state or quality of being light hearted or cheerful _____

6. a mode of behaviour or way of thought peculiar to an individual _____

7. the condition of being anonymous _____

8. concise and exact use of words in writing _____

9. for a very short time, soon _____

10. the state or fact of being likely to be influenced or harmed by a particular thing _____

11. the quality of being so delicate or precise as to be difficult to analyse or describe _____

12. produce a humorously exaggerated imitation of an artist, writer or genre _____

13. serving as a desirable model, very good _____

14. the state of being famous or well known for some bad quality or deed _____

15. moderately good, satisfactory _____

16. the quality of evoking a keen sense of sadness or regret _____

© Valerie Marett
Coroneos Publications

Australian Homeschooling #569
Successful Spelling 8

Unit 33: -ive, -ite

Look up the meaning and then learn these words.

conclusive	connive	derivative	elusive
figurative	furtive	interrogative	introspective
invective	pejorative	prerogative	provocative
receptive	reflective	repulsive	retrospective
tentative	vindictive	contrite	depict
erudite	expedite	incite	plebiscite

-ite makes adjectives and nouns meaning "connected with or belonging to."
-ive makes adjectives from verbs, meaning "pertaining to, tending to; doing, serving to do"

Etymology or Word Origin—erudite
Erudite comes from the Latin *eruditus* "learned, accomplished, well-informed," past participle of *erudire* "to educate, teach, instruct, polish," literally "to bring out of the rough," from assimilated form of *ex* "out" + *rudis* "unskilled, rough, unlearned."

The prefix re– means back, again, e.g., report, realign.

A. In the space below write the spelling words that contains the prefix re-.

1. _____ 2. _____ 3. _____

4. _____

B. Think carefully and then divide the following words into syllables.

1. provocative _____ 2. invective _____

3. interrogative _____ 4. incite _____

5. introspective _____ 6. provocative _____

7. tentative _____ 8. pejorative _____

9. receptive _____ 10. conclusive _____

C. Write an antonym for each word below.

1. retrospective _____ 2. contrite _____

3. repulsive _____ 4. vindictive _____

Choose a word from your spelling list that fits each definition below. Find the word in the word search and highlight it. Afterwards highlight the remaining spelling words. Every word from your spelling list is included.

E	V	I	T	A	G	O	R	R	E	T	N	I	T	X
V	F	I	N	W	P	S	E	T	C	I	P	E	D	E
I	E	N	E	T	I	R	T	N	O	C	L	V	E	D
T	V	V	T	P	R	E	R	O	G	A	T	I	V	E
A	I	E	I	K	I	O	O	R	J	W	E	T	I	R
R	S	C	C	N	P	X	S	C	F	S	R	P	T	I
U	U	T	N	V	N	A	P	P	D	N	U	E	C	V
G	L	I	I	S	D	O	E	O	E	H	D	C	I	A
I	E	V	I	S	U	L	C	N	O	C	I	E	D	T
F	P	E	J	O	R	A	T	I	V	E	T	R	N	I
R	E	F	L	E	C	T	I	V	E	J	E	I	I	V
F	B	A	E	P	R	O	V	O	C	A	T	I	V	E
A	A	W	F	R	P	L	E	B	I	S	C	I	T	E
R	E	P	U	L	S	I	V	E	V	I	T	R	U	F
E	V	I	T	A	T	N	E	T	I	D	E	P	X	E

1. given to examining or observing one's mental and emotional state _____

2. looking back on or dealing with past events or situations _____

3. arousing intense distaste or distrust _____

4. expressing contempt or disapproval _____

5. having or showing a strong or unreasoning desire for revenge _____

6. insulting, abusive or highly critical language _____

7. making happen sooner or accomplished more quickly _____

8. something which is based on another source _____

9. a right or privilege exclusive to a particular individual or class _____

10. attempting to avoid notice or attention, particularly because notice might bring trouble or retribution _____

11. encourage or stir up violent or unlawful behaviour _____

Other words found in the word search are: elusive, reflective, interrogative, conclusive, contrite, depict, connive, provocative, figurative, receptive, tentative, plebiscite, erudite.

Unit 34: more -ic,

Look up the meaning and then learn these words.

acoustic	anabolic	anaemic	analgesic
authentic	bombastic	cataclysmic	catastrophic
charismatic	choleric	democratic	diuretic
dogmatic	eccentric	ecliptic	ecstatic
egotistic	esoteric	hallucinogenic	metabolic
palaeontologic	pedantic	sadistic	sarcastic
sceptic	spasmodic	sporadic	thermodynamic

Etymology or Word Origin—cataclysmic

Cataclysmic is the adjectival form of cataclysm which comes from the Greek *kataklysmos* "deluge, flood, inundation," from *kataklyzein* "to deluge," from *kata* "down" + *klyzein* "to wash."

The prefixes cat-, cata– and cath– mean down, with, e.g., catalogue, catheter.

A. In the space below write the spelling word that contains the prefix cat-. Find an other words with the prefixes cat-, cata– and cath–.

1. _____   2. _____   3. _____

The prefix ec– means out of, outside, e.g., echo, ecstacy.

B. In the space below write the two spelling words that contain the prefix ec-.

1. _____   2. _____

The prefix dem– and demo– mean people, populace, population, e.g., democracy, demagogue.

C. In the space below write the spelling word that contains the prefix demo-. Find two other words with the prefixes dem– or demo-.

1. _____   2. _____   3. _____

The prefix meta- means beyond, change, e.g., metaphor.

D. In the space below write the spelling word that contains the prefix meta-. Find two other words with the prefix meta-.

1. _____   2. _____   3. _____

E. On a separate sheet of paper write the spelling words from exercises A-D. Divide the words into syllables.

A. Change the following words to adverbs.

1. sporadic _____   2. ecstatic _____

2. dogmatic _____   4. sadistic _____

B. From your spelling list choose 6 words that have scientific or geographical meanings, e.g., aeronautic.

1. _____   2. _____   3. _____

4. _____   5. _____   6. _____

C. Find a spelling word that fits each definition below.

1. high sounding words with little meaning _____

2. excessively concerned with minor details or rules _____

3. drug acting to relieve pain _____

4. a person likely to question or doubt accepted opinions _____

5. bad tempered, irritable _____

6. a great circle on the celestial sphere representing the sun's apparent path during the year _____

7. occurring or done in brief, irregular bursts _____

8. occurring at irregular intervals or in only a few places _____

9. marked by or given to using irony to mock or convey contempt _____

10. deriving pleasure from inflicting pain or humiliation on others _____

11. relating to sound or sense of hearing _____

12. a branch of physics concerned with heat and temperature and their relation to energy and work _____

13. involving or causing great damage or suffering _____

14. a drug causing causing increased passing of urine _____

© Valerie Marett
Coroneos Publications

Australian Homeschooling #569
Successful Spelling 8

Unit 35: Revision

Revise these words.

acrimony	aeronautic	bombastic	brevity
choleric	concomitant	derivative	ecstatic
epiphany	equanimity	frugality	furtive
idyllic	incite	introspective	munificent
nonchalant	notoriety	parsimony	pedantic
poignant	prerogative	provocative	repugnant

A. Complete the meaning of the following prefixes:

1. The prefixes co-, cog-, col-, coll-, com-, con-, cor- mean _____ _____.

2. The prefix trans- means _____.

3. The prefix sub- means _____.

4. The prefix re- means _____.

5. The prefix meta- means _____.

6. The prefixes pen- and pend- mean _____.

7. The prefixes il-, im-, in- and ir- mean _____.

8. The prefixes cat-, cata- and cath- mean _____.

9. The prefix dem- and demo- mean _____.

10. The prefix ec- means _____.

B. Complete these rules:

1. If "y" is the only _____ at the end of a word of more than _____the "y" says "___."

2. -ite makes _____ and _____ connected with or belonging to.

3. -ive makes _____ from _____, meaning "pertaining to, tending to; doing, serving to do."

A. Solve this crossword.

Across
1. feeling or expressing overwhelming happiness or joy
4. displaying great generosity
6. inward-looking
7. the state of being famous for bad deeds
8. excessively concerned with minor details or rules
9. bad tempered or irritable

Down
2. naturally accompanying or following something
3. based on another source
5. related to the science or practice of building or flying aircraft.

B. Write a sentence using the words shown below:

1. incite: _____

_____

2. provocative: _____

_____

3. bombastic: _____

_____

Unit 36: con-

Look up the meaning and then learn these words.

concede	conceited	conceivable	concentric
conciliation	concoct	concourse	concur
condemn	condone	configure	confiscate
conflagration	confute	constraint	construe
consular	contagious	contemplate	contextualise
contingency	contravene	contrite	convoluted

Con- is used before a consonant other than b, h, l, p, r. It means fully, thoroughly, with.

Etymology or Word Origin—contrite

Contrite comes from the Latin *contritus*, literally "worn out, ground to pieces," past participle of *conterere* "to grind," from com "with, together" + *terere* "to rub" Used in English in figurative sense of "crushed in spirit by a sense of wrong doing or sin."

A. To help you learn the words divide the following into syllables.

1. conciliate _____

2. conceivable _____

3. contingency _____

4. conflagration _____

5. concur _____   6. contemplate _____

7. concourse _____ 8. condone _____

9. condemn _____   10. confiscate _____

11. concoct _____   12. contravene _____

B. Change the word to a noun by adding –tion or –ion. Be careful! Use your dictionary.

1. contrite _____   2. configure _____

3. contravene _____ 4. contemplate _____

5. contagious _____ 6. confiscate _____

A. State whether each word is a noun, verb or adjective.

1. condone _____
2. conciliation _____
3. contingency _____
4. configure _____
5. constraint _____
6. confute _____
7. convoluted _____
8. contravene _____
9. construe _____
10. configure _____

B. Find a spelling word that fits each definition below.

1. extremely complex and difficult to follow _____

2. the action of stopping someone being angry _____

3. planning for a possible event or circumstances that can not be predicted with certainty _____

4. capable of being imagined or grasped mentally _____

5. take or seize someone's property with authority _____

6. interpret in a particular way _____

7. an extensive fire that destroys a lot of property _____

8. place or study in context _____

9. express complete disapproval of, sentence to a particular punishment _____

10. be of the same opinion, agree _____

11. of or denoting circles that share the same centre _____

12. coiled, twisted, complex, intricate _____

13. think deeply and at length _____

14. accept behaviour that is considered wrong or morally reprehensible _____

15. excessively proud of oneself _____

16. feeling remorse at the recognition that one has done wrong _____

© Valerie Marett
Coroneos Publications

Australian Homeschooling #569
Successful Spelling 8

Unit 37: -in

Look up the meaning and then learn these words.

inadvertent	inane	inaptitude	incision
incursion	indecent	indenture	induce
inertia	inference	inflammatory	initially
innuendo	insomnia	integral	intervene
intestacy	intimation	intimidate	intractable
intertwine	intrepid	intrinsic	inure

in- means "into, in, on, upon."

Etymology or Word Origin—intractable

About 1500 A.D. intractable was used to mean "rough, stormy;" in 1540s it took on the meaning "not manageable." It came directly from Latin *intractabilis* "not to be handled, unmanageable."

A. Change the following words to adjectives:

1. intestacy _____

2. incision _____

3. inference _____

4. incursion _____

B. Change the following words to verbs:

1. inference _____

2. intimation _____

C. Change the following words to verbs:

1. inure _____

2. initially _____

3. intractable _____

4. intervene _____

D. Two words in your list can be used as a noun or a verb. Write them below.

1. _____

2. _____

E. Find two synonyms for each word below:

1. intrinsic _____ _____

2. integral _____ _____

3. innuendo _____ _____

© Valerie Marett
Coroneos Publications

Australian Homeschooling #569
Successful Spelling 8

B. Find a spelling word that fits each definition below.

1. lacking sense or meaning _____

2. not fitted or skilled in the area _____

3. to take part in something so as to alter a result or course of events _____

4. twist or turn together, connect or link _____

5. a tendency to do nothing or remain unchanged _____

6. a surgical cut made in skin or flesh _____

7. the action of making something known, especially in an indirect way _____

8. frighten to make a person do what one wants _____

9. offending against generally accepted standards _____

10. hard to control or deal with _____

11. accustomed to something, especially something unpleasant _____

12. an invasion or attack, especially a sudden or brief one _____

13. an elusive or oblique remark or hint, typically a suggestive or disparaging one _____

14. not resulting from or achieved through deliberate planning _____

15. belonging naturally, essential _____

16. too great or extreme to be expressed _____

17. a conclusion reached on the basis of evidence and reasoning _____

18. fearless, adventurous _____

19. the condition of an estate of a person who dies without making a valid will _____

20. succeeding in persuading or leading _____

Unit 38:

Look up the meaning and then learn these words.

abjure	abstruse	brusque	cajole
demagogue	demeanour	epicurean	eponym
etiquette	evince	exasperation	exhort
fracas	gourmand	haemorrhage	hedonist
hiatus	iconoclast	juxtapose	libertarian
maladroit	maelstrom	malapropism	misanthrope
opprobrium	ostracism	surveillance	umbrage

Etymology or Word Origin—etiquette

Etiquette came from the French *étiquette meaning* "prescribed behavior." It came from the Old French *estiquette* meaning "label, ticket." It appeared in France in 1750 and perhaps came from behavior instructions written on a soldier's billet for lodgings and/or small cards written or printed with instructions for how to behave properly at court.

The prefix mal- means bad or badly, e.g., malfunction, malady

A. In the space below write the spelling word that contains the prefix mal-. Find one other words with the prefixes mal-.

1. _____ 2. _____ 3. _____

The prefixes op-, ob-, oc- and of- mean toward, against, in the way, e.g., oppose, occur, offer, obtain.

B. In the space below write the spelling word that contains the prefix op-, ob-, oc- and of-. Find two other words with the prefixes op-, ob-, oc- and of-.

1. _____ 2. _____ 3. _____

The prefixes ab- and abs- mean away from, off, e.g., absolve, absent.

C. In the space below write the spelling words that contain the prefixes ab- or abs-.

1. _____ 2. _____

The prefix de- means from, down, away, to do the opposite, reverse, against, e.g., detach, derange, deploy.

D. In the space below write the spelling words that contain the prefixes de-.

1. _____ 2. _____

Choose a word from your spelling list that fits each definition below. Find the word in the word search and highlight it. Afterwards highlight the remaining spelling words.

E	M	A	L	A	P	R	O	P	I	S	M	V	N	B
Q	G	V	P	N	A	E	R	U	C	I	P	E	R	W
U	D	A	W	A	R	O	A	B	S	T	R	U	E	E
I	E	T	H	I	P	J	M	A	S	U	S	A	L	T
V	M	K	R	R	B	E	N	I	J	Q	S	B	F	I
O	A	U	T	A	R	T	N	B	U	I	I	P	R	Q
C	G	M	I	T	H	O	A	E	C	S	J	N	A	U
A	O	I	A	R	D	N	M	O	N	T	U	G	C	E
T	G	M	O	E	B	L	N	E	J	R	X	O	A	T
I	U	P	H	B	L	O	T	I	A	O	T	U	S	T
O	E	T	I	I	C	S	R	F	F	H	A	R	U	E
N	G	X	U	L	O	K	T	P	F	X	P	M	T	N
G	E	G	A	R	B	M	U	R	P	E	O	A	A	D
F	M	S	I	C	A	R	T	S	O	O	S	N	I	D
M	T	B	K	R	U	O	N	A	E	M	E	D	H	W

1. a noisy disturbance or quarrel   _____

2. outward behaviour or bearing   _____

3. a situation or state of confused movement or violent turmoil   _____

4. the mistaken use of a word in place of a similar sounding one, often with amusing effect   _____

5. an escape of blood from a ruptured blood vessel   _____

6. a political leader who seeks support by appealing to popular desires and prejudices rather than rational arguments   _____

7. a person who attacks or criticises cherished beliefs or institutions   _____

8. harsh criticism or censure   _____

9. place or deal with close together for contrasting effect   _____

10. offence or annoyance   _____

Find the other spelling words also hidden in the word search: epicurean, etiquette, ostracism, gourmand, exhort, abjure, abstruse, hiatus, brusque, hedonist, libertarian.

Unit 39

Look up the meaning and then learn these words.

amateur	assuage	camaraderie	chameleon
epithet	expunge	impinge	panacea
paradigm	parenthesis	perfidy	perturbed
placebo	plethora	puerile	sanguine
sequester	silhouette	subterfuge	succinct
surfeit	verbatim	vestige	vicissitude

Etymology or Word Origin—panacea

Panacea comes from Latin *panacea*, "a herb that would heal all illnesses", from Greek *panakeia* "cure-all," from *panakes* "all-healing," from *pan-* "all" + *akos* "cure". In English it was used from 1540 to mean a universal remedy.

The prefix para- means beside, e.g., paradox, paramedic.

A. In the space below write the spelling word that contains the prefix para-. Find two other words with the prefix para-.

> 1. _____   2. _____   3. _____

The prefix per– mean through, or intensive, e.g., permit, perforate.

B. In the space below write the spelling words that contains the prefix per-.

> 1. _____   2. _____

The prefixes ver- or very- mean true, e.g., verdict, verify.

C. In the space below write the spelling word that contains the prefix ver-. Find two other words with the prefix ver-.

> 1. _____   2. _____   3. _____

The prefixes vic– or vicis– mean change, substitute, e.g., vicarious.

D. In the space below write the spelling word that contains the prefix vicis-. Find two other words with the prefix vicis-.

> 1. _____   2. _____   3. _____

E. Use the word below in a sentence.

> 1. plethora: _____

A. Look up in a dictionary and write the definition of each word bellow.

1. paradigm: _____

2. silhouette: _____

3. sanguine: _____

4. chameleon: _____

5. verbatim: _____

6. assuage: _____

7. camaraderie: _____

8. puerile: _____

B. Choose a word from your spelling list to fit each definition below:

1. an excessive amount of something _____

2. advance over an area belonging to someone or something else _____

3. briefly and clearly expressed, especially of something written _____

4. an adjective or phrase expressing a quality or attribute regraded as characteristic of the person mentioned _____

5. the state of being deceitful and untrustworthy _____

6. a word or phrase inserted as an explanation which is grammatically complete without it, and in writing usually marked by brackets, dashes or commas _____

7. a trace or remnant of something that is disappearing or no longer exists _____

8. a change of circumstances or fortune, typically one that is unpleasant _____

9. obliterate or remove completely something that is unpleasant _____

Unit 40: Important Foreign Terms

These foreign words are in common usage. Look up the meaning of the word or phrase. Write the meaning below. Learn to spell the list.

1. à la carte: _____

2. ad hoc: _____

3. ad nauseam: _____

4. alias: _____

5. bona fide: _____

6. carte blanche: _____

7. caveat emptor: _____

8. curriculum vitae: _____

9. crème de la crème: _____

10. de facto: _____

11. de rigeur: _____

12. double entendre: _____

13. ergo: _____

14. erratum: _____

15. ethos: _____

16. faux pas: _____

17. habeas corpus: _____

18. ibid: _____

19. impromptu: _____

20. in absentia: _____

21. in extremis: _____

22. in lieu: _____

Look up the meaning of the word or phrase. Write the meaning below. Learn to spell the list.

1. joie de vivre: _____

2. kudos: _____

3. laissez-faire:_____

4. magnum opus: _____

5. modus operandi: _____

6. non sequitur: _____

7. per annum: _____

8. per capita: _____

9. persona non grata: _____

10. phobia: _____

11. piece de resistance: _____

12. prima facie: _____

13. pro rata: _____

14. quid pro quo: _____

15. quod erat demonstrandum (QED): _____

16. re ipsa locuitor: _____

17. sangfroid: _____

18. status quo: _____

19. sub judice: _____

20. subpoena: _____

21. terra nullius: _____

22. tete a tete: _____

23. vis a vis :_____

Spelling Test

Parent to administer test. 1 point per word. Pass: 70%

abhorrent	hypoxia	soliloquy
aberrance	idiosyncrasy	subpoena
acrimonious	ignominious	substantiate
aesthetic	ignominy	subtlety
androgynous	impertinent	sycophant
apocryphal	inauguration	synecdoche
acquiescence	inconsequential	truculent
asphyxiation	incorrigible	ubiquitous
audacious	interrogative	vehemently
belligerent	interspersion	vindictive
bombastic	intractable	vituperation
brusque	introspective	vociferous
cacophonous	irascible	
calumny	litigious	
camaraderie	loquacious	
cataclysmic	magnanimous	
catastrophic	malevolent	
cognizance	malfeasance	
coherent	maelstrom	
complaisant	misanthrope	
conceptualise	munificent	
condescension	obfuscation	
conflagration	onomatopoeia	
conscientious	ophthalmology	
contemporaneous	palaeontologic	
contravene	paraphernalia	
controversial	paroxysm	
convoluted	pejorative	
denigrate	perspicacity	
depreciation	pertinacious	
depredation	plebiscite	
derogatory	plethora	
dichotomy	poignant	
disparity	precedence	
embezzlement	preferential	
ephemeral	presumptuous	
equanimity	promulgate	
exacerbate	provocative	
feasible	recalcitrance	
gesticulation	repugnant	
gregarious	retrospective	
haemorrhage	rudimentary	
heinous	sequestration	
hyperbole	silhouette	

Australian Homeschooling #569
Successful Spelling 8

Answers Successful Spelling 8

Page 4, Unit 1
A. Change to an adjective

2. illogical
3. austere
4. long
5. solemn
6. disparate
7. gullible
8. congruous
9. perverse
10. equanimous

B. Definitions

1. **affinity:** a natural liking of something or someone else.

2. **proclivity:** a tendency to choose or do something regularly; an inclination or predisposition towards a certain thing

3. **probity:** the quality of strong moral principles; honesty

4. **congruity:** a quality of agreement and appropriateness; harmonious

Page 5
A. Antonym & Synonym
(Answers my vary. A suggestion is given.)

1. **duplicity:** deceit, dishonesty (s) sincerity, truthfulness (a)

2. **perversity:** tenacity, abstinence (s) irresolution (a)

3. **congruity:** symmetry, coherence (s) irregularity, difference (a)

4. **probity:** integrity, rectitude (s) deceit, dishonesty (a)

5. **alacrity:** promptitude, quickness (s) lethargy, apathy (a)

B. Choose word to match definition

1. longevity
2. gullibility
3. austerity
4. perversity
5. disparity
6. duplicity
7. authenticity
8. alacrity

C. Divide into syllables

1. au/then/tic/ity
2. dis/par/ity

3. e/qua/nim/ity
4. guil/li/bil/ity

D. Prefix meaning

1. **pro:** in favour, for, forward
2. **dis:** not, opposite of, reverse
3. **per:** through, by, for each

Page 6, Unit 2

A. Meaning of words

1. **ophthalmology:** the branch of medicine concerned with the study and treatment of disorders and diseases of the eye.

2. **histology:** the study of the microscopic structure of tissue.

3. **morphology:** the study of the form, shape or structure of a particular thing.

4. **pathology:** the science and study of the causes and effects of diseases, especially the branch of medicine that deals with the laboratory examination of samples of body tissue for diagnostic or forensic purposes.

B. Noun or Adjective

1. adjective
2. adjective
3. adjective
4. noun
5. adjective
6. noun

C. Definition and Sentence

1. **complementary:** combining in such a way as to enhance or emphasize the qualities of another.
   Parent to mark sentence.

2. **complimentary:** making a statement praising or approving someone. Parent to mark sentence.

Page 7

A. Word meaning

1. cursory
2. rudimentary
3. tautology
4. corollary
5. desultory
6. quandary

© Valerie Marett
Coroneos Publications

Australian Homeschooling #569
Successful Spelling 8

Answers Successful Spelling 8

B. Noun, Adjective or Both
1. adjective
2. noun
3. noun
4. adjective
5. adjective
6. noun

C. Add ending
1. literary
2. laboratory
3. necessity or necessary
4. anthropology
5. dormitory
6. abnormality
7. military
8. archaeology
9. civility

D. List word for antonym
1. cursory
2. peremptory
3. derogatory
4. rudimentary
5. desultory
6. conciliatory

Page 8, Unit 3
A. Divide into syllables
1. el/egy
2. pith/y
3. trich/o/to/my
4. de/lin/quen/cy
5. dis/crep/an/cy
6. ig/no/min/y

B. Adjectival form
1. hierarchical
2. clement
3. discrepant
4. hegemonic
5. ignominious
6. discrepant

C. Change to verbs
1. calumny
2. entreat
3. consist

D. Prefix meaning
1. **con-** fully
2. **tri-** three
3. **en-** put into, make, provide with, surround with

Page 9
A. Fit word to definition
1. hegemony
2. oxymoron
3. ignominy
4. delinquency
5. dichotomy
6. soliloquy
7. elegy
8. hierarchy
9. trichotomy

B. Antonym
1. ruthlessness, strictness
2. similarity
3. agreement
4. irregularity, inconsistency
5. demand

C. Synonym from spelling list
1. ignominy
2. discrepancy
3. calumny
4. soliloquy
5. pithy

Page 10 Unit 4
A. Definition
1. synecdoche
2. eponym
3. paroxysm
4. aneurysm
5. cynicism
6. synecology
7. androgynous
8. idiosyncratic
9. pseudonym
10. cataclysm

B. Change the form of the word
1. vilification or vilifier
2. idyll
3. cryptically
4. mythological or mythologic

Page 11
A. Adjectival form
1. stereotypical
2. aneurysmal
3. mythological
4. cataclysmic
5. eponymous
6. cynical

Answers Successful Spelling 8

B. Write the noun form of the word
1. cyclic
2. vilification
3. idyll
4. dynamic

C. Meaning of prefixes
1. **an-**; not, without, before
2. **crypto-**: concealed, secret
3. **pseudo-**: purporting to be, not really so
4. **dys-**: bad or difficult
5. **cata-**: (before a vowel or h) down or downwards, wrongly, badly
6. **ac-**: to, towards, near
7. **syn-**: synonymous, with, together, alike
8. **dynam-**: power

D. Meaning of suffixes
1. **-ism**: doctrine, belief, action or conduct
2. **-ic**: having to do with, having the nature of, caused by, similar to
3. **-ology**: a subject of study or interest, characteristic of word or language
4. **-onym**: name

E. Divide into syllables
1. dys/func/tion/al
2. idio/syn/crat/ic
3. an/drog/y/nous
4. syn/ec/col/ogy

Page 12, Revision
A. Complete the rules
1. abstract noun   adjective
2. contain a vowel
3. only   one   long e sound
4. the study of

B. Synonym
1. stereotype
2. pseudonym
3. authenticity
4. desultory
5. rudimentary
6. gullibility
7. cataclysm
8. peremptory
9. controversy
10. duplicity

C. Antonym
1. controversy

2. perversity
3. complementary
4. derogatory
5. duplicity
6. proclivity

D. Make words
Any of the following: plea, men, come, complement, money, tent, meant, carp, complete, comment, car, maple, pane, tar, net, pleat, tame, part, party, yarn, yam, plenty, place, male, lean, lame, pen, plot, late, pea, compare, camp, yet, pace, art, part, pleat, plate, coal, moment, trample, commentary, pole, lent, mental, metal, mean, team, late, let, lament, name, me, map, Mary, Peter, ten, tape, trap, palm, Pam, cement, lent, lean, mole, lame, lot, ample, pace, tale, tare, mare, many, temple, meal, mop

Page 13
A. Crossword

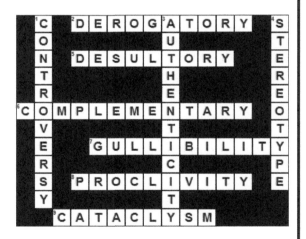

B. Plurals
1. proclivities
2. oxymorons

C. Plural rules for y
add "s"   change "y" to "i" and
add "es"   "s"

Page 14
A. ab-
1. aberration
2. abrogation

B. Prefix Meanings
1. **ad-, ap-:** to, toward, near, in addi-

Answers Successful Spelling 8

to, by

2. **com-, con-:** with, together, altogether
3. **de-:** from, down, away, to do the opposite, reverse, against
4. **equi-:** equal
5. **gest-:** carry or bear
6. **homo-:** same
7. **in-, im-:** into, on, near, towards

C. Base word
1. depreciate
2. improvise
3. abrogate
4. homogenise

Page 15
A. Unscramble word
1. adjuration
2. gesticulation
3. depredation
4. attrition
5. asphyxiation
6. equivocation
7. conflagration
8. abrogation
9. compunction
10. derogation
11. approbation
12. contradiction
13. improvisation
14. diminution
15. adulation

B. Change to a verb
1. homogenise
2. exemplify
3. improvise
4. gesticulate
5. asphyxiate
6. adjure

Page 16, Unit 7
A. Divide words into syllables
1. per/son/i/fi/ca/tion
2. super/an/nu/a/tion
3. sum/mar/i/sa/tion
4. pre/dil/ec/tion
5. se/quest/ra/tion
6. in/au/gur/a/tion

B. Change to a verb
1. marginalise
2. inundate
3. ossify
4. stagnate

5. obfuscate
6. mature
7. proliferate
8. invalidation

C. Change to adjectives
1. ostentatious
2. proliferative
3. inaugural
4. injunctive
5. vituperative
6. invalidate

D. Unscramble the words
1. requisition
2. trepidation
3. volition
4. invalidation

Page 17
A. Synonym
1. summarisation
2. volition
3. ostentation
4. injunction
5. vituperation
6. requisition
7. invalidate

B. Definition
1. inundation
2. obfuscation
3. sequestration
4. predilection
5. inauguration
6. trepidation
7. ossification
8. proliferation
9. superannuation
10. personification
11. maturation
12. stagnation
13. ostentation
14. vituperation
15. volition

Page 18, Unit 8
A. Adjectives, Adverbs
1. specific   specifically
2. egocentric   egocentrically
3. felicitous   felicitously
4. veracious   veraciously
5. ethnic   ethnically
6. perspicacious perspicaciously
7. tenacious   tenaciously

B. Adjective and Noun
1. chronological   chronology
2. inquisitive   inquisitiveness
3. vicarious   vicariousness
4. expeditious   expeditiousness
5. vehement   vehemence
6. sympathetic   sympathy

N.B. Sometimes, but not always, adjectives are changed to nouns by adding "ness." "Ness" can not be added to adverbs. Poor language skills have led to words like "wellness," but despite common usage, this is incorrect since well is an adverb.

Page 19
Definition
1. veracity
2. misogynist
3. capacity
4. chronologically
5. vehemently
6. tenacity
7. egocentricity
8. eccentricity
9. extensively
10. vicariously
11. felicity
12. labyrinth
13. ethnicity
14. ferocity

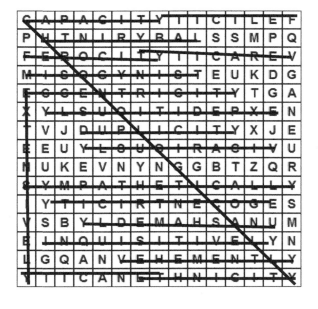

Page 20, Unit 9
A. Definition
1. philanthropic
2. euphemism
3. neophyte

4. phalanx
5. phlegmatic
6. choreography
7. sycophant
8. periphery
9. diaphanous
10. atrophy
11. euphonious
12. apocryphal

Page 21
A. eu-
Any order
1. euphemism
2. euphonious
3. euphoria

B. Prefix dem-
1. demographic
Answers will vary for 2 and 3.
Suggestions:
2. democracy
3. demagogue

C. Suffixes -ous, -eous, -ious
Order may vary
1. cacophonous
2. diaphanous
3. euphonious

D. Syllables
1. e/phem/er/al
2. phil/an/thropic
3. neo/phyte
4. para/pher/nal/i/a
5. cac/o/phon/ous
6. em/phat/ic
7. a/poch/ry/phal
8. per/i/pher/y

E. Noun
1. cacophony
2. philanthropy
3. apocrypha
4. demography
5. phlegm
6. sophisticate

F. Sentences
Parent to mark.

Page 22, Unit 10
A. Complete
1. -sion   t   te
2. good, well, luckily, happily

Answers Successful Spelling 8

3. adjective   having the quality of, relating to
4. away from, off
5. people   populace   population

B. Latin or Greek plural
1. algae
2. phenomena
3. parentheses
4. indices
5. media
6. nuclei

C. Syllables
1. se/quest/ra/tion
2. phen/om/en/a
3. ob/fus/ca/tion
4. ges/tic/u/la/tion

Page 23

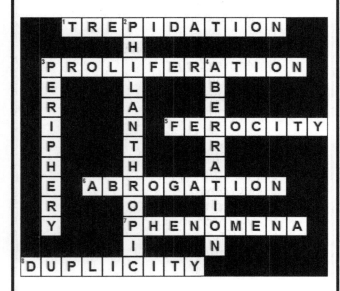

A. Crossword puzzle
B. Synonyms
Answers may vary. Suggestions are given

1. **obfuscation:** complicate, confuse, muddy
2. **expeditiously:** speedily, efficiently, rapidly
3. **gesticulation:** gesture, wave, indication
4. **ostentation:** flamboyance, pompousness, exhibition

Page 24, Unit 11
A. Prefix con-, col-
Any order
1. colloquial
2. congenial
3. conspiratorial
4. controversial

B. Meaning
Any order
1. **colloquial:** used in an ordinary or familiar conversation
2. **congenial:** liked because they have qualities or interests similar to one's own
3. **conspiratorial:** a surreptitious plan formulated in secret
4. **controversial:** likely to give rise to public disagreement

C. Prefix pre- or pro-
Any order.
1. precedential
2. preferential
3. proprietorial

D. Homonyms
precedential   presidential

Page 25
A. Definitions
1. preferential
2. inconsequential
3. quintessential
4. potential
5. colloquial
6. controversial
7. proprietorial
8. adversarial

B. Prefix in-
1. inconsequential
2. insubstantial

C. Definitions
1. actuarial
2. deferential
3. congenial
4. tangential
5. potential

D. Change to an adverb
1. insubstantially
2. torrentially
3. conspiratorially
4. colloquially

Answers Successful Spelling 8

Page 26, Unit 12
A. Prefix dis-
Any order.
1. disparate
2. disseminate
3. dissipate

B. Definition dis- words
1. disseminate
2. dissipate
3. disparate

C. ex- words and meaning
Any order.
1. **exacerbate:** make a problem or situation worse
2. **expiate:** make amends or reparation for wrong doing
3. **expostulate:** express strong disapproval or disagreement

D. Syllables
1. ac/cul/tur/ate
2. cor/rob/or/ate
3. com/men/sor/ate
4. em/u/late

Page 27
A. Complete chart
1. collaboration (n)
   collaborationist (adj)
   collaboratively (adv)
2. debilitation (n)
   debilitative (adj)
3. delineation (n)
4. enumeration (n)
   enumerable (adj)
5. attenuation (n)
   attenuate or attenuated (adj)

B. Definitions
1. denigrate
2. baccalaureate
3. debilitate
4. acculturate
5. emulate
6. actuate
7. expostulate
8. delineate
9. enervate
10. contraindicate
11. decimate
12. commensurate

C. Write the definition
1. **attenuate:** reduce the force of, effect or value of
2. **exacerbate:** make a bad situation worse
3. **collaborate:** individuals who work together for a common purpose

Page 28, Unit 13
A. Prefixes in-, im-
Any order.
1. importunate
2. inchoate
3. indeterminate
4. indiscriminate
5. instigate
6. inveterate

B. Sentences
Parent to mark.

C. Complete the chart
1. subjugation (n)
   subjugable (adj)
2. scintillating (adj)
   scintillatingly (adv)
3. expurgation (n)
   expurgatorial (adj)
4. relegation (n)
   relegable (adj)
5. palliative or palliation (n)
   palliative (adj)
   palliatively (adv)

Page 29
Wordsearch

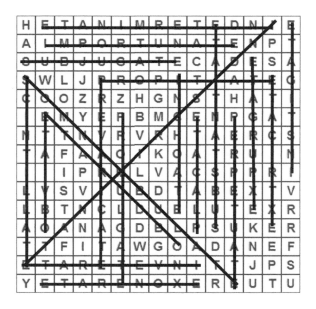

Answers Successful Spelling 8

1. exonerate
2. subjugate
3. inveterate
4. inchoate
5. placate
6. expurgate
7. substantiate
8. instigate
9. promulgate
10. obdurate
11. obviate
12. importunate
13. propitiate
14. prevaricate

Page 30, Unit 14
A. hydro-
Any 3, any order.
1. hydrology
2. hydroponics
3. hydrofoil

B. hypo-
Any order.
1. hypodermis
2. hypotension
3. hypothesis
4. hypoxia

C. hyper-
1. hyperbole
2. hyperthermia
3. Parent to mark.

D. Adjectival form
1. expulsive
2. secessional
3. hysteric
4. dispersible
5. hygienic
6. impressionable

Page 31
A. hy- words
1. hydrate
2. hypodermis
3. hyphen
4. hypothesis
5. hyperbole
6. hydroponics
7. hydrology
8. hypoxia
9. hyena
10. hysteria
11. hybrid
12. hydraulic

B. Write definition
1. **digression:** a temporary departure

from the main subject in speech or writing.
2. **effusion:** an act of talking or writing in an unrestrained way
3. **preclusion:** to prevent the presence, existence or occurrence of; to exclude or debar from something
4. **derision:** contemptuous abuse or mockery

Page 32, Unit 15-Revision
A. Complete
1. not, into, near or towards
2. not, opposite of, reverse, separate, deprive of, away
3. out of, away from, lacking or former
4. over, usually implying excess or exaggeration
5. for, forward
6. having to do with water
7. fully
8. with or together
9. under, below, slightly
10. before   before, forward
11. two or more words having the same spelling or pronunciation but having different meanings

B. Use a word
1. obviate
2. vacillated

Page 33
A. Solve the crossword puzzle.

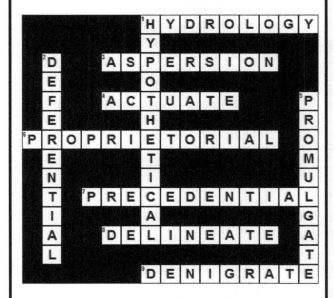

B. Divide into syllables
1. quint/es/sent/ial
2. ex/pur/gate

© Valerie Marett
Coroneos Publications

Australian Homeschooling #569
Successful Spelling 8

Answers Successful Spelling 8

Page 34, Unit 16
A. Meaning of erroneous
incorrect, arising from an error, mistake

B. Words related to water
Any order
1. aqueous
2. crustaceous

C. Synonym for immediately
Any order
1. instantaneous
2. simultaneous

D. Words where g says j
Any order
1. advantageous
2. courageous

E. Sentences
Parents to mark.

Page 35
A. Definitions
1. contemporaneous
2. vitreous
3. consanguineous
4. extemporaneous
5. heterogeneous
6. predaceous
7. erroneous
8. aqueous
9. discourteous
10. nauseous
11. spontaneous
12. advantageous

B. Noun form
1. spontaneity
2. advantage
3. instantaneity
4. discourteousness
5. contemporaneity
6. predaceousness
7. extraneousness
8. erroneousness

C. Antonym
Answers may vary.
1. cowardly, faint-hearted
2. mannered, respectful
3. accurate, correct
4. harmful, unprofitable
5. rehearsed, planned

Page 36, Unit 17
A. prefix per—
Any order
1. pernicious
2. perspicacious

3. pertinacious

B. Prefix un-
1. unsuspicious
2 & 3. Answers will vary.

C. Prefix mal-
malicious
intending to do harm

D. Noun and adjectival form
1. avarice (n)
   avariciously (adv)
2. tenacity (n)
   tenaciously (adv)
3. pertinacity (n)
   pertinaciously (adv)
4. mendacity (n)
   mendaciously (adv)

Page 37
A. Write the definition
1. **avaricious:** having or showing an extreme greed for wealth or material possessions
2. **fallacious:** based on a mistaken belief
3. **rapacious:** aggressively greedy or grasping
4. **officious:** assertive of authority in a domineering way; intrusively enthusiastic in offering help or advice
5. **auspicious:** conducive to success; giving or being a future sign of success; characterised by success

B. Word to fit definition
1. voracious
2. pertinacious
3. loquacious
4. capricious
5. precocious
6. vivacious
7. luscious
8. mendacious
9. perspicacious
10. audacious
11. malicious
12. tenacious
13. pernicious

Page 38, Unit 18
A. Prefix co-
1. copious
2 & 3. parent to mark

B. Prefix im- and in-
not, into, near or towards Any order.
1. impecunious

© Valerie Marett
Coroneos Publications

Australian Homeschooling #569
Successful Spelling 8

Answers Successful Spelling 8

1. impecunious
2. impervious
3. insidious

C. Syllables
1. ac/ri/mon/ious
2. ig/no/min/ious
3. greg/ar/ious
4. im/pec/un/ious
5. de/let/er/ious
6. multi/far/ious
7. cop/ious
8. lit/ig/ious

D. Sentence
Parents to mark.

Page 39
Definitions
1. disputatious
2. conscientious
3. gregarious
4. acrimonious
5. fastidious
6. impecunious
7. multifarious
8. contentious
9. insidious
10. egregious
11. impervious
12 atrocious
13. licentious

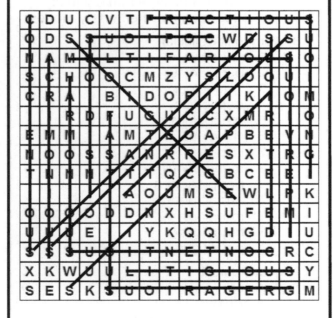

Page 40, Unit 19
A. Prefix per-
sacrilegious
Parent to check.

B. Prefix pre- and pro-
Any order.
1. precarious
2. prodigious

C. Prefix super-
supercilious: looking or behaving as though one is superior to another.

D. Adverbs
1. obsequiously
2. surreptitiously
3. repetitiously
4. superciliously
5. obnoxiously
6. precariously

Page 41
A. Write a sentence
Parents to mark.

B. Definition
1. temerarious
2. amoeba
3. penurious
4. meritorious
5. vicarious
6. spurious
7. obnoxious
8. subpoena
9. nefarious
10. sanctimonious
11. salubrious
12. precarious
13. noxious
14. prodigious

Page 42, Unit 20
A. Complete the following:
1. **un-**: not, against, opposite
2. **pre-**: **pur-**: before
3. **per-**: through, thoroughly or intensive
4. **co-**: with, together
5. **sacr-**: sacred
6. **mal-**: bad, badly
7. **pro-**: for or forward
8. **super-**: above, beyond, to a great or extreme degree, of a higher kind

B. Write sentences
Parents to mark.

Answers Successful Spelling 8

Page 43
A. Crossword Puzzle

B. Change the word
1. avariciousness or avarice (n) avariciously (adv)
2. extraneousness (n) extraneously (adv)
3. discourtesy (n) discourteously (adv)

Page 44, Unit 21
A. Prefix ex-
1. exigent
2. expedient

B. Prefix ambi-
1. ambivalent
2. & 3. Parent to mark.

C. Prefix ab- or abs-
1. abhorrent
2 & 3. Parent to mark.

D. Sentences
Parent to mark.

Page 45,
A. Draw a line to the definition
1. e. insurgent
2. i. coherent
3. a. ebullient
4. k. augment
5. f. impertinent
6. m. ambivalent
7. o. fraudulent
8. b. intransigent
9. g. abhorrent
10. n. incumbent
11. l. exigent
12. c. decadent

13. j. deterrent
14. h. evanescent
15. d. embezzlement

B. Complete the chart
1. abhorrence (n) abhor (v)
2. denouncer (v)
3. constituent or constituency (n) constitute (v)
4. effervescence (n) effervesce (v)

Page 46, Unit 22
A. Prefix re-
Any order
1. reticence
2. resplendent
N.B. reminiscent is rem– not re-

B. Prefix ob-
Any order.
1. obsolescent
2. opalescence
3. Parent to check.

C. Prefix di-
1. divergence
2. & 3. Parent to check.

D. Divide into syllables
1. mu/nif/i/cent
2. cre/dence
3. pru/ri/ent
4. ac/quies/cence
5. nas/cence
6. turb/u/lence
7. bel/lig/er/ence
8. rem/in/i/cent

Page 47
A. Meaning
1. divergence
2. acquiescence
3. nascence
4. prurient
5. malevolent
6. reticence
7. ambience
8. opalescence
9. truculent
10. eloquence
11. precedence
12. concurrence
13. resplendence
14. reminiscent
15. indolence

B. Difference between word meanings
Parent to check.

Australian Homeschooling #569
Successful Spelling 8

Answers Successful Spelling 8

C. Adjectival and adverbial form
1. turbulent (adj)
   turbulently (adv)
2. somnolent (adj)
   somnolently (adv)
3. belligerent (adj)
   belligerently (adv)

Page 48, Unit 23
A. Prefix ab-
1. aberrance
2. abeyance
3. Parent to check. Make sure the word contains a prefix and not just a syllable.

B. Prefix for-
1. forbearance
2 & 3. Parent to check.

C. Prefix re-
Any order.
1. recalcitrance
2. reconnaissance
3. Parent to check.

D. Antonymn
Answers may vary slightly
1. moderation, temperance
2. restraint, simplicity
3. very few, minimum
4. stranger, unfamiliarity
5. obedience, tractability
6. lethargy, sluggishness
7. doubt, uncertainty
8. ignorance

Page 49
Crossword

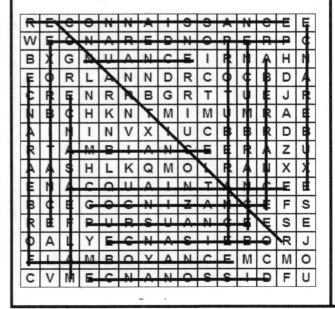

1. reconnaissance
2. aberrance
3. cognizance
4. exorbitance
5. recalcitrance
6. acquaintance
7. malfeasance
8. nuance
9. protuberance
10. exuberance
11. flamboyance

Page 50, Unit 24
A. Prefix con-
Any order.
1. congruous
2. conspicuous
3. contemptuous
4. contiguous

B. Prefix in-
Any order.
1. ingenuous
2. incongruous
3. indigenous
4. innocuous

C. Prefix magn-, mono-
1. magnanimous
2. monogamous

Sentence: Parent to check.

Page 51
A. Noun
1. abstention
2. meticulousness
3. contemptuousness
4. magnamity
5. heinousness
6. ingeniousness or ingenuity
7. garrulity or garrulousness
8. conspicuousness
9. horrendousness
10. anomaly

B. Antonym
1. unambiguous
2. distant
3. harmful
4. advantageous
5. quiet
6. inconspicuous
7. intelligent, sensible
8. justifiable, necessary

Australian Homeschooling #569
Successful Spelling 8

9. respectful
10. affable, good-natured

C. Definition
1. fatuous
2. incongruous
3. anomalous
4. contemptuous
5. monogamous
6. heinous
7. garrulous
8. clamorous
9. credulous

Page 52, Unit 25 Revision
A. Meaning of prefixes
1. back or again
2. two, twice, double
3. away from, off
4. love, like or liking
5. with or together
6. one
7. both ways
8. away from, off
9. out of, away from, lacking, former
10. toward, against, in the way
11. not   into, on, near, toward
12. great
13. before

B. Antonym
Answers may vary slightly
1. co-operative, peaceful
2. mean-spirited, selfish
3. harmful, obnoxious
4. uniformity, conformity

Page 53
A. Crossword

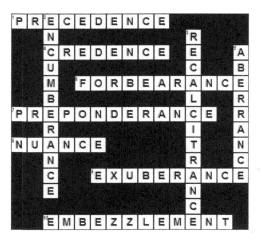

B. Write a sentence.
Parent to mark.

Page 54, Unit 26
A. Prefix sol-
1. solicitous
2. Parent to mark.

B. Prefix pre-
1. preposterous
2. precipitous
3. presumptuous

C. Long u sound
Any order
1. ubiquitous
2. unanimous
Not unction—short u sound

D. Syllables
1. ob/strep/er/ous
2. pre/sump/tu/ous
3. que/rul/ous
4. u/nam/i/mous
5. scru/pu/lous
6. post/hum/ous
7. plat/i/tud/in/ous
8. rau/cous

E. Sentence
Parent to check.

Page 55
A. Definitions
1. onerous
2. presumptuous
3. slanderous
4. ubiquitous
5. preposterous
6. scurrilous
7. platitudinous
8. superfluous
9. obstreperous
10. unctuous
11. vociferous
12. querulous
13. scrupulous
14. raucous
15. posthumous
16. solicitous
17. unanimous
18. preposterous
19. tempestuous
20. precipitous

Page 56 Unit 27
A. Syllables
1. al/luv/i/al
2. plag/i/a/rise

Answers Successful Spelling 8

3. ego/tis/ti/cal
4. un/cont/ra/vers/ial
5. para/dox/i/cal
6. dia/bol/i/cal
7. far/ci/cal
8. eth/e/re/al

B. Change verb to noun
1. enfranchisement
2. scrutiny
3. category
4. plagiary
5. conceptualism
6. aggrandizement

C. Change to adverbs
1. egotistically
2. ethereally
3. inimically
4. empirically
5. diabolically
6. prejudicially
7. effectually
8. potentially

D. Write a sentence.
Parent to mark.

Page 57
A. Definition
1. diabolical
2. aggrandize
3. inimical
4. farcical
5. paradoxical
6. plagiarise
7. enfranchise
8. ethereal
9. ostracise
10. accrual
11. empirical
12. actuarial
13. ethereal
14. rebuttal
15. scrutinize
16. alluvial
17. jurisdictional
18. categorise
19. conceptualise

Page 58, Unit 28
A. Prefix acer-
acerbic   Parent to mark.

B. Prefix aero-
1. aeronautic
Answers may vary
2. aerial

3. aerodrome
C. Write answer
Answers may vary. Parent to check.
1. aeronaut
2. lethargy
3. antagonist
4. aesthete
5. enigma
6. laconically
7. antagonist

Page 59

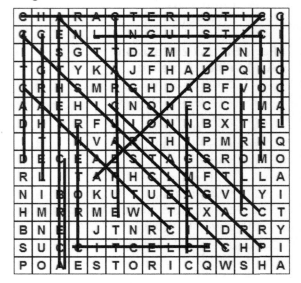

Definitions
1. characteristic
2. altruistic
3. eclectic
4. antagonistic
5. bureaucratic
6. didactic
7. enigmatic
8. aesthetic
9. lethargic
10. ascerbic

Page 60 Unit 29
A. Revision: sufixes
1. **con-:** with, together   contemptible
2. **in-:** into, on, near, towards, not
incontrovertible, incorrigible,
inexorable, inimitable or
ineffable, inexhaustible
3. **dis-:** not, opposite of, reverse
separate, deprive of, away
discernible
4. **ex-:** out of, away from, lacking,
execrable

5 **im-:** not   impeccable
6 **re-:** back, again   redoubtable
not reprehensible suffix is rep

B. Antonym
Answers may vary slightly
1. limited wear
2. intangible, imperceptible
3. imperceptible
4. flawed, imperfect
5. admirable
6. sceptical, wary

C. Synonym
Answers may vary slightly
1. habitual, hardened
2. impressionable
3. awful, atrocious
4. loathsome, abhorrent
5. superficial
6. deplorable
7. achievable
8. daunting
9. unquestionable
10. inexpressible

Page 61
A. Write the definition
Answers may vary slightly
1. **discernible:** perceptible, noticeable
2. **inimitable:** so good or unusual that it can not be copied
3. **irascible**: having a tendency to be easily angered
4. **ineffable:** too great or extreme to be expressed
5. **submersible**: able to go under the water
6. **reprehensible:** deserving condemnation or censure

B. Find a word to fit the definition
1. redoubtable
2. inexorable
3. gullible
4. contemptible
5. impeccable
6. inexhaustible
7. ostensible
8. susceptible
9. incontrovertible
10. incorrigible
11. despicable
12. execrable

C. Divide into syllables
1. con/tempt/ible

2. rep/re/hens/ible
3. in/im/it/able
4. feas/ible
5. a vowel

Page 62, Unit 30
A. Complete the meaning
1. bitter, sour, sharp
2. alone
3. point or dot
4. air, of aircraft

B. Syllables
1. vit/ri/ol/ic
2. ob/strep/er/ous
3. im/pec/ca/ble
4. pre/sump/tu/ous
5. di/dac/tic
6. plag/i/ar/ize
7. act/u/ar/ial
8. scur/ril/ous

C. Antonym
Answers may vary slightly
1. fanciful
2. tragic, humourless
3. sombre, calm
4. respectful

D. Synonym
Answers may vary.
1. common, routine
2. credulous, trusting
3. choleric, grouchy
4. artificial, counterfeit

E. Definition actuarial
Parent to mark.
relating to the work of compiling and analysing statistics.

Page 63
Crossword

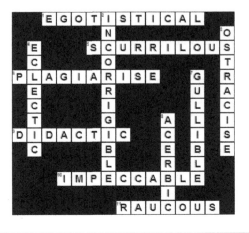

B. Sentences
Parent to check

Page 64 Unit 31
A. Prefix co-,com-, con-
Any order
1. coagulant
2. complaisant
3. concomitant

B. Prefix in-
Any order
1. incoherent
2. indolent
3. increment

C. Prefix pen-
1. penchant
2. & 3. Parent to mark.

D. Prefix trans-
1. transcendent
2. & 3. Parent to mark.

E. Syllables
1. co/ag/u/lant
2. trans/cen/dent

Page 65
A. Definitions
1. poignant
2. indolent
3. complaisant
4. penchant
5. adherent
6. desiccant
7. benevolent
8. repugnant
9. flagrant
10. concomitant
11. increment
12. petulant
13. incoherent
14. quotient
15. escarpment

B. Write a sentence
Parent to mark.

Page 66, Unit 32
A. Syllables
1. ac/cept/a/bil/ity
2. blas/phem/y
3. id/io/syn/cras/y
4. e/piph/an/y
5. poig/nan/cy
6. mo/men/tar/ily
7. haught/y

8. ar/bit/rar/y

B. Prefix sub-
1. subtlety
2. & 3. Parent to mark.

C. Prefixes iim-, in-,
Any order
1. implicitly
2. integrity
Sentence—Parent to mark.

Page 67
A. Change to verb
1. implicit
2. subtle
3. poignant
4. frugal
5. subtle
6. notorious

B. Definitions
1. criticality
2. integrity
3. parsimony
4. apathy
5. gaiety
6. idiosyncrasy
7. anonymity
8. brevity
9. momentarily
10. susceptibility
11. subtlety
12. parody
13. exemplary
14. notoriety
15. acceptibility
16. poignancy

Page 68, Unit 33
A. prefix re-
Any order.
1. receptive
2. reflective
3. repulsive
4. retrospective

B. Syllables
1. pro/voc/at/ive
2. in/vect/ive
3. in/ter/rog/at/ive
4. in/cite
5. intro/spec/tive
6. provocative
7. ten/ta/tive

Answers Successful Spelling 8

8. pe/jor/at/ive
9. re/cept/ive
10. con/clu/sive

C. Write an antonym
Answers may vary slightly.
1. prospective
2. unrepentant, defiant
3. alluring
4. forgiving, kind-hearted

Page 69, Find words

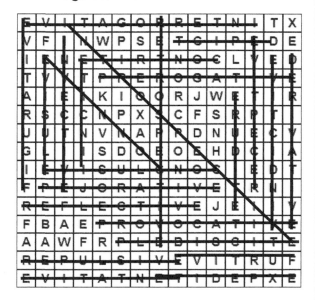

1. introspective
2. retrospective
3. repulsive
4. pejorative
5. vindictive
6. invective
7. expedite
8. derivative
9. prerogative
10. furtive
11. incite

Page 70, Unit 34
A. Prefixes cat-, cata- and cath-
1. catastrophic
2. cataclysmic
3. Parent to mark.

B. Prefix ec-
Any order.
1. eccentric
2. ecstatic   not eclyptic which has a long e sound not ec-

C. Prefixes dem-, demo-
1. democratic

2. & 3. Parent to mark.

D. Prefix meta-
1. metabolic
2. & 3. Parent to mark.

E. Syllables
Any order.
1. cat/a/stroph/ic
2. ec/cen/tric
3. ec/stat/ic
4. dem/o/crat/ic
5. met/a/bol/ic

Page 71
A. Adverbs
1. sporadically
2. ecstatically
3. dogmatically
4. sadistically

B. Geographic or scientific words
Any 6. Any order.
1. metabolic
2. thermodynamic
3. palaeontologic
4. cataclysmic
5. anabolic
6. ecliptic
7. anaemic
8. analgesic

C. Definitions
1. bombastic
2. pedantic
3. analgesic
4. sceptic
5. choleric
6. ecliptic
7. spasmodic
8. sporadic
9. sarcastic
10. sadistic
11. acoustic
12. thermodynamics
13. catastrophic
14. diuretic

Page 72 Unit 36
A. Prefixes
1. with, together
2. across, beyond, change
3. below, secretly
4. back, again
5. beyond, change
6. to hang
7. not

8. down, with
9. people, populace, population
10. out of, outside

B. Complete these rules
1. vowels   one syllable   "ee"
2. adjectives   nouns
3. adjectives   verbs

Page 73
A. Crossword

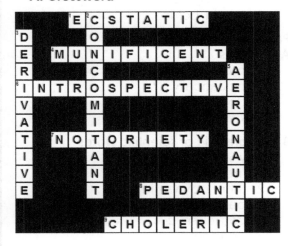

B. Sentences
Parents to mark.

Page 74, Unit 37
A. Syllables
1. con/cil/i/a/tion
2. con/ceiv/able
3. con/tin/gen/cy
4. con/fla/gra/tion
5. con/cur
6. con/tem/plate
7. con\course
8. con/done
9. con/demn
10. con/fis/cate
11. con/coct
12. con/tra/vene

B. Add -tion
1. contrition
2. configuration
3. contravention
4. contemplation
5. contagion
6. confiscation

Page 75
A. Noun, verb or adjective
1. condone—verb

2. conciliation—noun
3. contingency—noun
4. configure—verb
5. constraint—noun
6. confute—verb
7. convoluted—adjective
8. contravene—verb
9. construe—verb
10. configure—verb

B. Definition
1. convoluted
2. conciliate
3. contingency
4. conceivable
5. confiscate
6. construe
7. conflagration
8. contextualise
9. condemn
10. congenial
11. concentric
12. convoluted
13. contemplate
14. condone
15. conceited
16. contrite

Page 76, Unit 37
A. Change to Adjectives
1. intestate
2. incisive
3. inferential
4. incursive

B. Change to verbs
1. inference
2. intimate

C. Change to nouns
1. inurement
2. initial (can also be an adj. or verb)
3. intractableness
4. intervention

D. Both a noun and a verb
Any order.
1. innuendo
2. indenture

E. Synonyms
Answers may vary
1. inherent   inseperable
2. essential   fundamental
3. insinuation   implication

Answers Successful Spelling 8

Page 77
Definitions
1. inane
2. inaptitude
3. intervene
4. intertwine
5. inertia
6. incision
7. intimation
8. Intimidate
9. indecent
10. intractable
11. inure
12. incursion
13. innuendo
14. inadvertent
15. intrinsic
16. inflammatory
17. inference
18. intrepid
19. intestacy
20. induce

Page 78, Unit 38
A. Prefix mal-
1. malapropism
2. Parent to mark.

B. Prefix op-, ob-, oc– and of–
1. opprobrium
2 & 3. Parent to mark.

C. Prefixes ab-, abs-
Any order.
1. abjure
2. abstruse

D. Prefixes de-
Any order.
1. demagogue
2. demeanour

Page 79

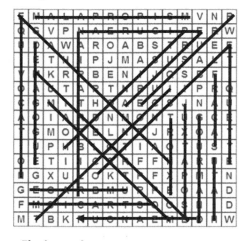

Find words

1. fracas
2. demeanour
3. maelstrom
4. malapropism
5. haemorrhage
6. demagogue
7. iconoclast
8. opprobrium
9. juxtapose
10. umbrage

Page 80, Unit 39
A. Prefix para-
1. paradigm
2 & 3. Parent to mark.

B. Prefix per-
Any order.
1. perfidy
2. perturbed

C. Prefix ver-, vis-, visi-
1. verbatim
2 & 3. Parent to mark.

D. Prefix ver-
1. verbatim
2 & 3. Parent to mark.

E. Sentence
Parent to mark.

Page 81
A. Write definition
Answers may differ slightly.
1. **paradigm**: a typical answer or pattern of something
2. **silhouette**: the dark shape and outline of someone shown in restricted light
3. **sanguine**: optimistic or positive, especially about a difficult situation
4. **chameleon**: a person who changes their opinion or behaviour according to a situation
5. **verbatim**: in exactly the same words as were used originally
6. **assuage**: satisfy, or make an unpleasant feeling less intense
7. **camaraderie**: mutual trust and friendship among people who spend a lot of time together
8. **puerile**: childishly silly and immature

© Valerie Marett
Coroneos Publications

Australian Homeschooling #569
Successful Spelling 8

Answers Successful Spelling 8

B. Word to fit definition:
1. surfeit
2. impinge
3. succinct
4. epithet
5. perfidy
6. parenthesis
7. vestige
8. vicissitude
9. expunge

Page 82, Unit 40
Foreign Terms
1. according to/from the menu
2. created or done for a specific purpose as necessary
3. an argument or discussion that continues to the point of being nauseating
4. a false or assumed identity
5. genuine, without intention to deceive
6. complete freedom to act as one wishes
7. buyer beware (the principle is that the buyer alone is responsible for checking reliability and suitability of goods prior to purchase)
8. a brief account of a person's education, qualifications and previous occupations, usually for a job (resume)
9. the best person or thing for a particular job
10. existing or holding a specific position, whether by legal right or not
11. required by etiquette or current fashion
12. a word or phrase open to two interpretations, one of which is often rude or risqué
13. therefore
14. correction of a published error
15. the characteristic spirit of a culture, era or community as manifested in its attitudes and aspirations
16. an embarrassing or tactless act in a social situation
17. a writ requiring a person under arrest to be brought before a court or judge to secure the person's release unless lawful grounds are shown for their detention
18. an abbreviation used to mean in the same source in textual references to a quoted work which has been mentioned in a previous reference
19. done without being planned or rehearsed
20. while not present at the event referred to
21. at the point of death; in an extremely difficult situation
22. instead of, in place of

Page 83
Foreign Terms
1. a cheerful enjoyment of life
2. praise and honour received for an achievement
3. the policy of leaving things to take their own course; lack of interference of government in the workings of a free market
4. the most important work of an artist or writer
5. a particular way or method of doing something
6. a conclusion or statement that doesn't logically follow from the last statement
7. each year
8. for each person (literally per head)
9. person who is not welcome somewhere
10. an extreme or irrational fear or aversion to something
11. the most important or impressive item
12. accepted as so until proved otherwise
13. proportional
14. a favour or advantage given in return for something
15. that which is to be demonstrated (usually used at the end of a math proof) to indicate the proof is complete
16. the thing speaks for itself, self evidently
17. the ability to stay calm in difficult circumstances
18. the existing state of affairs, especially regrading political or social issues
19. being considered by a court of law therefore not to be discussed publicly
20. a summons ordering a person to attend court
21. nobody's land
22. a private conversation between two people
23. in relation to, as compared with

© Valerie Marett
Coroneos Publications

Australian Homeschooling #569
Successful Spelling 8